Teesside
at
War

Malcolm Race
additional research by
Clive Hardy

1. This photograph shows some of the damage caused at South Bank during Teesside's first air raid. Though censored, the official caption reads: 'These cottagers are searching the debris of their houses wrecked after a Nazi plane had dropped bombs in the North Riding of Yorkshire. Eight civilians were injured. They are the first civilians to be injured in raids on England.'

First published 1989 by
Archive Publications Ltd
Carrington Business Park
Urmston, Manchester M31 4DD
in association with
The Evening Gazette
Gazette Buildings
Borough Road
Middlesbrough
Cleveland TS1 3AZ

Printed and bound in the United Kingdom by
Netherwood Dalton & Co Ltd, Huddersfield

© 1989 Text Malcolm Race and Clive Hardy
© 1989 RAF Thornaby Text David Thompson
© 1989 Photographs as per acknowledgements

ISBN: 0-948946-42-3

2. Famous New Zealand woman aviator Jean Batten attended the handing over of six ambulances from the Durham Miners' Federation to the Anglo-French Ambulance Corps for service in France, in May 1940. In the centre is the Mayor of Middlesbrough, Councillor Sir William Crosthwaite.

Introduction

When the Second World War broke out in 1939, many feared that the Teesside area, with its concentration of vital heavy industry, would quickly become a *front line* target. In the event, as with the north-east generally, Teesside was fortunate and never experienced devastation on the scale suffered by places like London, Coventry, Liverpool and Bristol. How did it escape more widespread destruction?

Sir Arthur Lambert, who was Regional Commissioner for the Northern Region throughout the war (covering Northumberland, Durham and the North Riding of Yorkshire), tried to give the answer in a personal message of thanks which he sent to those who had been involved in Civil Defence measures early in 1945.

Firstly, he put it down to the strength of the area's defences — fighters, guns, balloon barrage and searchlights, aided by the Royal Observer Corps. The 'crushing defeat' inflicted on the Luftwaffe when it launched its only large-scale daylight raid on the north-east coast on 15 August, 1940 (75 bombers were brought down) established a tradition which was well maintained, Sir Arthur claimed. "Enemy pilots held the area in great respect, this being confirmed by a German pilot captured near London late in the war who, when asked what he and his fellow pilots thought of our defences, replied 'that they had been engaged fiercely in most parts of Britain, but above all others the one they disliked attacking was the north-east coast.'"

The second reason, suggested Sir Arthur, "seems to be a geographical one, that is the deep and tortuous valleys of our principal rivers which destroy their value as guiding lines; on many occasions the coastal ports were hit, but the raiding aircraft got hopelessly lost and scattered when probing inland."

He went on: "Thirdly, the natural industrial haze constantly obscuring the vital targets was an enormous protection and this was increased during moonlight periods by the artificial smoke screen which was first experimented with and adopted on the River Tyne."

Nevertheless, Teesside and the surrounding area — what is now the County of Cleveland — did have its share of attacks, casualties, damage, drama, tragedy — and heroism. Even the remote parts of East Cleveland did not escape.

The pattern of life for Teessiders remained much the same during 1940-42 and into 1943. The vast majority of attacks came during the night. Warning sirens wailed — an eerie sound which never failed to give a sharp twist to the stomach, no matter how often one heard it. Families would rouse themselves blearily from their beds and make their way to the shelter in the garden or take cover as best they could downstairs, or perhaps join their neighbours in a communal shelter in the street or on nearby wasteland.

The drone of enemy aircraft overhead would be mixed with the crump-crump of bombs exploding and the roar of anti-aircraft guns — and, from July 1942 onwards, the even noisier and more terrifying rocket guns.

Emergency services would spring into action, air raid wardens, rescue and first-aid teams, firemen, firewatchers and the rest. As things quietened down and the enemy cleared our shore, the all-clear (one continuous note on the sirens) would pierce the silence. The raid was over. Time to return home and to bed to snatch a few hours' rest before another working day dawned.

Surprisingly, perhaps, the local record of those traumatic years and the story of what life was like under constant threat of air attack, has never been gathered together in one detailed and illustrated history. This book is an attempt to rectify that omission — and also to give some idea of the area's important industrial and military contribution to the war effort.

Acknowledgements

The author expresses his grateful thanks to the many people who have assisted in the preparation of this book.

They include Peter Darling, editor of the *Evening Gazette*; Albert Stockwell, former Town Clerk of Thornaby; Mrs Jennifer Hopkins, daughter of the late Teddy Baxter (former chief photographer of the *Evening Gazette*, who took many of the photographs reproduced); Cleveland County's recently-retired Librarian and Leisure Officer Frank Regan, his successor Janet Barker, and his former deputy, the late Leslie Still, together with Reference Library staff in the county; Cleveland County Archivist David Tyrell and his staff; ICI Ltd's public relations staff and Mr Julian Phillips, former intelligence manager; the public relations and records office staff of British Steel; Mrs Ethel Gaunt, Bill Taylor and Norman Ferguson of Middlesbrough; Stan Haggarth of Thornaby; the late Councillor Bill Herlingshaw, of Grangetown and the late Councillor Gordon Hodgson, also of Grangetown; Tom Sowler, the Stockton historian; Clive Hardy for designing the book and also for tracking down military photos and information; John Holt, of Yarm; journalist Derek Hebden and his father, former rescue service officer Reginald Hebden; David Bayliss of Thornaby; Mr David Thompson of Billingham; Mr Harold Thompson and Mrs Norma Pearson; the Dorman Museum, Middlesbrough; Kirkleatham Museum; George Levett and Zetland Museum, Redcar; Mrs Grace Picknett (for permission to reproduce wartime Redcar photographs); Jim Ellison, for assistance over F Hills and Sons' war effort; Ron Brunskill, formerly of Smith's Dock; John Proud, chairman of the Teesside branch of the World Ship Society — and his book, *Seahorses of Tees*, telling the story of Tees Towing Co Ltd; Tees Towing Co itself for permission to reproduce the picture of tugs towing a caisson; Norman Nicholson of Fairfield, Stockton, for Power-Gas Corporation Ltd photographs; and Stanley Ward, of Carlin How. I should also like to thank The Green Howards Regimental Museum, Richmond for their enthusiastic help with photographs and information.

It has been invaluable to be able to refer to the *Evening Gazette's* files and book of wartime cuttings and especially the end-of-war summaries written by the then chief reporter, Tom Stake, who was a colleague of the author. Last, but far from least, thanks go to the present *Gazette* photographic staff for their considerable help — and forebearance!

September 1939

The evacuation of British towns and cities began on 31 August 1939 but it was on 8 September that there was something of a mass exodus from industrial Middlesbrough. Under the government's official scheme, a total of 6,227 people were evacuated from the town. They comprised 4,963 unaccompanied schoolchildren, 650 mothers with children, 34 expectant mothers with 18 children, 9 handicapped adults and 553 teachers and helpers.

The evacuation areas for this first scheme were in the more isolated parts of the North Riding and South West Durham — and it became a matter of great concern to the emergency committee when large numbers returned home within a matter of a few weeks, homesickness apparently proving a stronger emotion than fear of German bombs.

In Middlesbrough, schools in so-called vulnerable areas were closed indefinitely and it was made clear that pupils unwilling to be evacuated would receive no schooling. There were some strange anomalies; for example, Middlesbrough High School (then in the red-brick building at the corner of King Edwards Road and Albert Road) was considered to be in danger but Kirby Secondary School apparently was not, despite the fact that pupils of both often lived in the same street!

The author was one of the thousands who took part in the exodus and for this article he has also drawn on the experiences of one of his schoolmasters, Mr G Wilson Smith.

With the familiar little cardboard boxes containing our gas masks slung round our necks, name labels fluttering from lapels and cases in hand, pupils and staff of the High School gathered, bewildered and not a little apprehensive, on Middlesbrough railway station. A special train was to take us via York and Malton to Scarborough. Oddly enough, however, children from Scarborough were evacuated inland!

On arrival in the resort groups of ten or twenty boys, accompanied by one or two masters, walked to their billets in boarding houses and hotels on South Cliff. The proprietors of these 'mini boarding schools' were paid £1 a week for each adult and eight shillings (40p) for each child to feed us. About a dozen of us, with a master, Mr 'Chuck' Hewson, found ourselves shepherded to a boarding house run by two elderly ladies in a quiet street behind the main shopping parade. Our hosts were doubtless as apprehensive as we were and not overjoyed to have a gaggle of boisterous boys deposited on their somewhat spartan guest house.

Food was not too plentiful and home comforts few — although this was not the case in some of the larger hotels. Schooling proved a problem initially. We were to use a building which had housed Scarborough Girls' High School until their new school was ready. It was void of any furniture so for two or three weeks, until arrangements could be made for the transport of our own desks and books, there was no school — and no lessons.

The weather was fine at first and long hours were spent on the beach, round the harbourside and at the bathing pools. Mr Wilson Smith recalls that one morning at about eleven o'clock he was on a crowded beach on the North Side, enjoying the sunshine, when a plane flew over the sea.

3. The opening shots of World War Two. The German battleship *Schleswig-Holstein* bombards Polish fortifications at Westerplatte, near Danzig on 1 September 1939.

"Nobody took much notice till it was overhead and not at all high," he remembers. "Then, it was a German plane. It circled once and flew off again across the sea. No siren, no gunfire, no chase..."

Autumn passed and a cold, hard winter followed. Our main entertainments were a trip to the pictures or playing beat the waves on the rocks below the Spa — with many a resultant soaking.

I suffered a bout of conjunctivitis and returned home. The anticipated bombing attacks on industrial Teesside did not materialise and, as the months went by, boys from the school began to drift back to Middlesbrough. Soon, so many children had given up that schools in the town had to re-open including the High School which opened its doors for about half its usual complement of boys and staff. By April 1940 the whole school was back in its own familiar 'Alfred Waterhouse' building in the town centre.

With the fall of France, however, air raids did begin in earnest and early in the summer of 1940 a second evacuation was ordered, this time, in our case, to Upper Teesdale.

Once again we were treated to a mystery tour by train, and this time we ended up split between the three picturesque villages of Romaldkirk, Cotherstone and Lartington. No hotels or boarding houses here; we were billeted in homes, individually or in twos and threes.

Two of us were 'left over' after the initial allocation of billets and stayed temporarily with the stationmaster and his wife at their house near Cotherstone station.

We were finally 'posted' to the village grocer, elderly, slow-moving, Willie Hodgson, grey-haired and with a bushy moustache, who lived behind and over his tiny shop next to the Methodist Church in the main street (the shop has since been converted into a house).

A bachelor, keen fisherman and gardener, he had a housekeeper, Miss Margaret Douglas, a formidable figure,

4. 9 September 1939, Gateshead evacuees at Stokesley.

good hearted but quick of temper, forthright — and not to be crossed!

Their home was far removed from the neat, comfortable suburban semi I had left behind in Acklam. There were stone-paved floors, oil lamps, brass-knobbed bedsteads — and a primitive 'privy' down the garden.

We spent nearly two years there and despite the unfamiliar surroundings and complete change of routine it was not an unhappy time. Each day from Monday to Friday we travelled by train the few miles to Barnard Castle — over the now-demolished Deepdale Viaduct — to attend school in the unlikely surroundings of Bowes Museum, watched over by numerous marble busts and works of art.

We usually took a snack for mid-day, eating it in the museum grounds or cafe, although we often wandered into town. When the sinking of the German battleship *Bismark* was announced over the radio a number of us were tucking into baked beans on toast at a cafe in the main street. With us there was the headmaster, Mr 'Willie' Fletcher — and he immediately ordered extra sweets all round to mark the occasion.

The final bus to Barnard Castle each day carried a postbox and people waited at bus stops in the villages, not to board, but to hand over mail to the conductress.

On Sundays we attended services at the parish church in the morning and, under pressure from Miss Douglas, the Methodist Church in the evenings — with rural preachers rambling interminably through ad hoc prayers and fire-and-brimstone sermons.

The school Scout troop was revived by French master, Mr Alan 'Bill' Bream. The troop met on Saturday mornings at Lartington and held several summer holiday camps on land at Mr Brown's farm at Bowbank, in Lunedale, a mile or two from Mickleton.

The troop put together a sort of 'gang show' or revue and staged it in halls in the villages to raise money for the Red Cross. In conjunction with the indefatigable Miss Douglas — she was captain of the village Girl Guides as well as Methodist Sunday School superintendent — we organised a regular joint Scout-Guide collection of waste paper, storing it in a large stone barn overlooking the main village green. I still have copies of the *Teesdale Trekker*, a monthly duplicated magazine which the troop produced at Barney. Some of us went on to become runners for the Home Guard.

The Dunkirk evacuation was quickly followed by an influx of weary soldiers into Cotherstone to regroup and rest. One of them was Donald Thorne, well-known before the war as a broadcasting organist and he was invited to give a concert on the Methodist Church organ. I was asked to send a short report to the local weekly, the *Teesdale Mercury* and had the pleasure of seeing myself 'in print' for the first time, complete with unwarranted 'by-line'.

Mr Wilson Smith had been sent to Romaldkirk, where the Rector was billeting officer, and ended up occupying a small wooden hut on the common which had been vacated by previous evacuees. For meals he went to the nearby village pub.

"Country life for our town boys was quite a change," he comments. "Not a few of them profited, learning the names of birds, flowers, crops, bushes and trees, even how to distinguish between meadow and pasture, trying their hand at anything. Dialect overheard was puzzling...

"One boy who was doing his best to make friends with village folk was watching a farmer feed half-a-dozen bull calves and suggested, 'Won't it be nice when they're all giving you milk?' And the farmer: 'Nay, lad, t'ud be a roody miracle!'

"I remember the retired colonel of the DLI who had taken six of our boys into his home by the river and had a splendid influence on them. He filled any of their idle hours

5. Teesside evacuees leave their 'safe area' school after a morning session. The girls are carrying their gasmasks.

by teaching them the rudiments of infantry training in the large garden and from reports this was fun for all concerned."

Again, the evacuation began to collapse. After a time so many pupils had returned to Teesside that once again the school in Middlesbrough had to re-open. The establishment was run in two parts, with the headmaster in charge of operations at Barnard Castle and his deputy, Mr van der Heyden, looking after the Middlesbrough branch.

The staff had to be split — an unsatisfactory situation. The Teesdale contingent was to remain there almost till the end of the war but with my sixteenth birthday it was time for me to leave school. 'Bill' Bream helped me to draft a letter of application which, in the summer of 1942, resulted in my joining the *Evening Gazette* as a raw junior reporter.

In many ways the evacuation 'campaign' had been an exhilarating experience. If it did nothing else it left me with a lasting affection for Teesdale and its people — and an appreciation of the benefits of all the mod cons enjoyed by townies!

6. People weren't just evacuated *from* Teesside, they were also evacuated *to* it. Here a young mother from Gateshead arrives at her new home in New Marske, September 1939.

4th SEPTEMBER, 1939

GOLD MUST BE SOLD TO THE TREASURY

If you have any gold coins you must take it to the bank and sell it to the Treasury. Luxury imports, including motor-cars, clothing and perfumery, are banned.

These regulations were issued last night.

Residents in Britain must offer foreign securities and bullion, as well as gold coin, to their bankers.

Foreign exchange to be offered for sale includes currencies named by the Treasury from time to time. Those already named include:—

U.S. dollars, Guilders, Canadian dollars, Argentine pesos, Belgas, Swedish crowns, Swiss francs, Norwegian crowns and French francs.

Persons may apply through their bankers for permission to retain gold and foreign exchange required to meet contracts, made before the coming into force of these regulations, which provide for payments in gold or foreign exchange, for meeting the reasonable requirements of trade or business, or for reasonable travelling or other personal expenses.

Prices to be paid for gold and foreign exchange offered for sale are to be determined by the Treasury, and may be ascertained by inquiry at any bank.

The public should continue to transact business in foreign exchange and gold through the agency of their bankers.

Applications for exchange must be made on the appropriate form, and satisfactory evidence in regard to the transaction proposed must be produced in all cases.

Export of banknotes, gold, securities or foreign currency is prohibited except with permission.

Traders Must Insure

The order issued by the Board of Trade bans the imports, except under licence, of luxuries and goods of which there are sufficient home supplies.

This will conserve exchange for the additional purchases of other products required in war time.

The main categories of goods covered by the order are pottery and glass, cutlery, clocks and watches, textile goods and apparel (including footwear), optical chemicals and paints, soap, office machinery (including typewriters), motor-cars, musical instruments, perfumery and toilet requisites, toys and games and luxury foodstuffs.

Traders in Britain who sell goods liable to King's enemy risks must insure them under the War Risks Insurance Act.

This is part of a scheme which the Board of Trade has put into operation.

Liability of the Board as insurers will be determined by a policy of insurance issued in a form prescribed in the schedule of the War Risks (Commodity Insurance) (No. 1) Order.

Insurance is compulsory except where the value of a person's insurable goods does not exceed £1,000.

BILLETS BY ORDER, IF—

A FEW householders who have so far been unwilling to receive evacuees are asked not to force the Government to exercise compulsion.

Making this appeal yesterday, Sir Warren Fisher, the North-West Regional Commissioner, pointed out:

"It is not possible at present to say how long the billets will last.

"But all must be prepared for danger and hardship, and will be lucky if it takes no worse a form than receiving strangers into one's house.

"No war can be won under modern conditions unless the essential work of the towns can be continued in spite of air raids. This will be easier if the townspeople in dangerous areas can be relieved of anxiety for their young children.

"It is also of vital importance to preserve the lives of children, who will be the citizens of the next generation, so that householders in safer districts must take them in.

"Parliament has given powers to billet them compulsorily in the reception areas, and the Government is determined to use those powers if necessary."

HITLER BLAMES BRITAIN

HITLER, in messages to his Army of the West and to the German people yesterday, blamed Britain for the war.

He claimed that the Poles had "attacked" Germany, and that he was fighting to "establish peace." He added that he was on the way to the Eastern Front.

To his troops on the Western Front he said (according to the German News Agency, quoted by Reuter):—

"The British Government, driven on by those warmongers whom we knew in the last war, has resolved to let fall its mask and to proclaim war on a threadbare pretext.

"For months it (the British Government) has supported the Polish attacks against the lives and security of fellow-Germans and the rape of the Free City of Danzig," continued Hitler.

"In a Few Months"

"Now that Poland, with the consciousness of this protection, has undertaken acts of aggression against Reich territory, I have determined to blow up this ring which has been laid round Germany.

"Sections of the German Army in the East have now, for two days, in response to Polish attacks, been fighting for the establishment of a peace which shall assure life and freedom to the German people.

"If you do your duty, the battle in the East will have reached its successful conclusion in a few months, and then the power of the whole Nazi State stands behind you.

"As an old soldier of the world war, and as your supreme commander, I am going, with confidence to you, to the Army on the East."

"Unity or—" Threat

To the German people Hitler said the English "encirclement" policy was resumed when the "peaceful" revision of the Versailles Treaty seemed to be succeeding.

To this he added: "The same lying inciters appeared as in 1914."

Claiming that "as long as the German people was united it has never been conquered," Hitler uttered this threat:—

"Whoever offends against this unity need expect nothing else than annihilation as an enemy of the nation."

DUKE TAKES UP NAVAL POST

The Admiralty announces that Rear-Admiral His Royal Highness the Duke of Kent has taken up his war appointment.

Immediately after Mr. Chamberlain's dramatic broadcast to the nation, the Government yesterday announced a number of precautionary measures to prevent people crowding together and so increasing the casualty risks from air raids.

Instructions were given for the closing of all places of entertainment until further notice. In the light of experience it may be possible to open cinemas and theatres in some areas later. Included in the closure orders are indoor and outdoor sports gatherings where large numbers of people might be expected to congregate.

The following advice is given:—

Keep off the streets as much as possible; to expose yourself unnecessarily adds to your danger.

Carry your gas mask with you always.

Make sure every member of your household have on them their names and addresses clearly written. Do this on an envelope or luggage label and not on an odd piece of paper which may be lost.

Sew a label on children's clothing so that they cannot pull it off.

People are requested not to crowd together unnecessarily in any circumstances.

Churches and other places of public worship will not be closed.

All day schools in evacuation and neutral areas in England, Wales and Scotland are to be closed for lessons for at least a week from yesterday.

In the reception areas schools will be opened as soon as evacuation is complete.

Cinemas, Theatres Close to Cut Risks

PETROL IS RATIONED

PETROL rationing will be introduced, as from September 16. This was announced last night by the Secretary for Mines. Information as to how the public can secure their ration books will be announced to-day.

There are very substantial stocks of petrol in the country, but in the national interests the best use must be made of these supplies.

Petrol distributors have arranged to pool all their resources and, after the individual brands still in stock at garages and service stations have been sold by them at prices now ruling, one grade only of motor spirit will be supplied to the public.

This spirit will be called "Pool" motor spirit, and will be on sale, ex-pump, in England and Wales at 1s. 6d. a gallon.

Appeal to Owners

No change will be made in the price for the next fourteen days at least. From to-day no further supplies of individual brands will be made at garages and service stations.

For at least the same period of fourteen days there will be no change in yesterday's bulk prices to those commercial concerns who receive their supplies direct.

Owners and drivers of commercial vehicles are particularly asked to note that it will no longer be possible to allow commercial vehicles to call at petrol companies' depots for supplies.

The Government appeal to all owners of motor vehicles to use them only for essential purposes.

BANKS ARE SHUT TO-DAY

TO-DAY has been declared a limited Bank Holiday, affecting only banks. The arrangement applies to the Post Office Savings Bank and other savings banks.

This day will be used by the banks to complete their measures for adapting themselves to the emergency, and to-morrow morning the banks will be open for business.

The Treasury, in conjunction with the Bank of England, have taken all the steps needed to ensure that the banks (including the Post Office Savings Bank and other savings banks) will be amply supplied with currency.

Postal orders will be legal tender for the present, and Scottish and Northern Ireland banknotes will be legal tender in Scotland and Northern Ireland respectively.

AIR MAIL CURTAILED

Empire air mail services are from to-day restricted to two services weekly in each direction between the United Kingdom and Sydney and one weekly in each direction between the United Kingdom and Durban and between the United Kingdom and Kisumu.

Corresponding modifications will be made in the overseas connecting services operated by Imperial Airways.

Present arrangements under which first-class mail to certain countries is forwarded by Empire Air Mail services without surcharge will be suspended, and a surcharge will be imposed on all mail from the United Kingdom carried by air on the Empire routes.

Day-old Babies Leave

Three babies born only the previous day were among three trainloads of evacuees from London yesterday.

Accompanied by their mothers, they were driven in an ambulance from the station to a nursing home which has been taken over as a maternity home.

U.S. REFUGEES LEAVE LONDON

BETWEEN two and three thousand American refugees left London last night.

Many of them were destitute.

An American Embassy official said it might take ten days before sufficient ships to evacuate these people will have put in.

Mr. Joseph Kennedy, American Ambassador, has requested all American and other neutral steamship lines to provide all available ships, including freighters and tankers, for evacuation.

WARNINGS TO SHIPPING

The Board of Trade announces: "Shipping is hereby warned that all traffic proceeding through the Dover Straits must proceed through the Downs. Ships disregarding this warning do so at their own peril."

The Admiralty give notice that vessels entering the Firth of Forth must pass to the northward of Bass Rock. Vessels proceeding to the southward of Bass Rock will do so at their own peril."

Air Raid Precautions

It was in July, 1937, that the Home Office issued its first circular to all local authorities about the preparations they should make for the protection of the civilian population in the event of war.

Until February, 1938, the normal administrative machinery of Middlesbrough County Borough Council was used to prepare steadily growing precautionary arrangements requested by the government. On 22 February 1938, however, Councillor (later to become Sir William) Crosthwaite, chairman of the council's General Purposes and Parliamentary Committee, urged the appointment of a special sub-committee, with plenary powers, to take over the responsibility for air raid precautions (ARP) in the town.

This was agreed — and he requested and was given the unusual privilege of selecting the membership of the sub-committee. He chose Alderman John Wesley Brown, Alderman Emmanuel Spence, Councillor T K Briggs, Councillor R V C Gray, Councillor Tom Meehan and Councillor John W Welch to act under his chairmanship. The sub-committee met for the first time on 25 February.

The ARP Committee was to meet on forty occasions until on 5 September 1939, the Town Clerk, Mr Preston Kitchen, assumed duties as controller on Home Office instructions. At a meeting on 5 September the sub-committee decided it should meet henceforth at 10.15 every morning together with the chief officers in charge of the various services and should function as an emergency committee.

Among the ARP services for which the sub-committee became responsible were wardens, air raid warnings, nursing services, anti-gas training, provision and management of shelters, emergency hospital arrangements, evacuation, billeting, communal feeding, rest shelters, information services, war damage repair, the Auxiliary Fire Service (AFS), rescue services, control and reporting, casualty services, fire prevention (including emergency static supplies) and the decontamination service.

The committee continued to meet daily until 20 October 1939. By the time it was disbanded on 12 June 1945, it had met on 134 occasions, gathering at any time of the day or night as emergencies arose.

Providing shelters for 100,000 of the town's population was an enormous task, involving trenches, the basements of stores and some commercial buildings (requisitioned under emergency powers), surface shelters of brick or steel in the streets and open spaces — as well as accommodation for 19,000 schoolchildren at schools. These shelters were supplemented by Anderson shelters in the gardens of people's homes and later by Morrison shelters inside some homes.

One of the most vivid memories of Stockton historian Tom Sowler, in his role as a deputy head warden of central Stockton early in the war, concerned not an air raid but the venom displayed by a little old lady.

"I was asked to umpire an exercise in which a bomb was supposed to have dropped," he explained. "I had to make notes about how the emergency services responded. The incident was to happen in one of the small streets of packed terraced houses off Garbutt Street and I was standing there when a back door opened and an old lady emerged to see what was happening.

"When I told her, she remarked, 'If one of those German

8. At the height of the Czech Crisis in September 1938, war seemed inevitable. ARP plans were put into effect. Here air raid trenches are being dug on Clairville Recreation Ground.

parachutists comes here I will show you what I will do to him.' With that, she went into the coalhouse in the yard and brought out a piece of wood about the length of a cricket bat. It had a handle but the other end was flat and through it had been driven a collection of ugly, rusty old nails, anything from one to four inches long.

"This old lady said: 'If a German parachutist comes to my door he is going to get this lot in his clock.' I looked at this horrifying weapon and could only think of all the blood poisoning it would cause!"

The war intruded on Tom's wedding day at Holy Trinity Church, Stockton, on 22 July 1940. During the ceremony a warden dashed in to spread the word that a yellow alert had been notified. Had this been succeeded by a red alert, which would have meant the sirens sounding, Tom would have been expected to leave his bride and rush to his post. Fortunately, this did not materialise and the ceremony was completed.

His honeymoon at Keld, in Swaledale, was also interrupted — by an urgent message to report to Harold Soar, manager of Stockton labour exchange, "on a matter of national importance." It turned out that the summons was merely to try to persuade Tom, who was a schoolteacher, to take up a reserved occupation and so avoid being called up for the Forces. He spurned the idea and shortly afterwards received his call-up papers for the RAF.

Tom explained the Stockton ARP set-up: "When the war came," he said, "Stockton Council took over one large floor of what had been Blair's engine works in Norton Road (later Hills) as a headquarters. The borough was divided up into a number of areas and in charge of each was a councillor who was head warden," he explained. "The Stockton central area stretched from the High Street up Yarm Lane, across to Oxbridge railway bridge and down the railway, and back along Bishopton Lane to the High Street.

"Councillor Stoddart, a butcher, was head warden for the area. He had a valuable asset — a Hillman Ten car — and was allowed petrol for it because of his official position. The official deputy head warden at that time was Sandy McLane, a shift worker at ICI.

"When hostilities were imminent we used Councillor Stoddart's car to deliver gasmasks to the various houses and hand them out. I had young women pleading with me for gasmasks for their babies — but at that stage we did not have any. We simply had large, medium and small gasmasks — and later, coloured 'Mickey Mouse' masks for young children. But we had none for the babies.

"Eventually babies' respirators were issued; they were like carry-cots with a canopy over and, as I remember, had a pump which had to be pressed by hand.

"Upon the outbreak of war, a chap came dashing round to our house, flung open the front door and yelled 'air raid alert, yellow'. A pregnant woman who happened to be passing by slumped to the ground in a faint and we brought her into the front room, revived her and gave her a cup of tea.

"Later, so as not to cause undue alarm, I had a bell fitted to my front door. Someone from the air raid post would come along and press the button if there was an alert and I would press a bell from my end to indicate I had heard. Wardens had a little brass plate fitted to their front doors saying 'air raid warden'.

"We had an air raid post in the boilerhouse of Mill Lane School, another in the schoolroom of Brunswick Methodist Church in Brunswick Street, and a third in the Mill Street West area — in the cellar of a small tailor's shop.

"We had regular wardens to man them round the clock and we had a system of runners — Rover Scouts — to call out others.

9. Sandbagging surrounds Middlesbrough Town Hall, September 1938.

"In the early days people used to object to being told to close doors because there was a light showing and also to being told to keep inside. They wanted to see what was going on. Strips of tape or paper had to be stuck, criss-cross fashion, on windows to minimise any blast damage — and car headlights had to be masked, with only a narrow slit left to emit light.

"I never got any uniform other than a helmet and gasmask. The uniforms came later."

Tom recalls that the cellars of the Empire Theatre (which stood where the Swallow Hotel and the shops beneath it are situated now and were reputed to be part of the dungeons of the former Stockton Castle) were opened up as a public air raid shelter.

It was also the shelter for children from Holy Trinity School, who used to practise making their way along Yarm Lane and down the steps into the cellars. Then it was decided the school should have its own underground shelters in the school yard.

Holy Trinity had extended its school yard in 1926 over part of the graveyard and the graves had to be disturbed. Tarpaulins were put out while workmen began taking up the bodies and it was arranged that the corpses would not be moved while children were about.

"One morning, however, I arrived early and found the headmaster already there. He was absolutely horrified because some of the kids had been under the tarpaulins, got out three or four skulls and were rolling them along the school yard. Later on," Tom added, "brick-built surface shelters were also erected so that another school could be accommodated."

BOROUGH OF STOCKTON-on-TEES

AIR RAID PRECAUTIONS

The Durham County Council is charged with the responsibility of making preparations for the protection of the civilian population of Stockton-on-Tees against the effects of any attack which may be made by hostile aircraft.

Stockton Borough Council is giving every possible assistance to the County Council in its task.

The scheme of precautions involves the enrolment of over **3,000** voluntary workers Of these approximately **1,000** have already enrolled.

An organisation has now been completed for the training of volunteers and the way is clear for large numbers of volunteers to be trained in the near future. **A RECRUITING CAMPAIGN IS BEING UNDERTAKEN BETWEEN the 3rd and 14th OCTOBER, 1938.**

In order that Stockton can be fully prepared to deal in every way possible with the dangers of hostile air attacks the A.R.P. Organisation **earnestly appeals** for volunteers to join the organisation.

It is far better to plan now and know what to do, than wait until war breaks out. Trained men and women would be essential in a National emergency, and it is necessary that thousands of residents of Stockton shall be prepared to offer their services **NOW.**

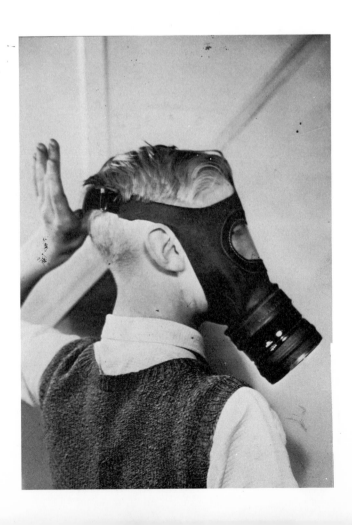

12. Stockton High Street, 1944. A static water tank is sited in the middle of the street.

13. Church Road, Stockton, 1944. The police station is the large building next to Hardy & Co.
The strange looking walls in front of the entrances are blast walls.

14. It looks dramatic, but in fact this scene, photographed at the corner of Russell Street and Dunning Street — outside the Municipal Buildings in Middlesbrough — shows schoolchildren trying out their gasmasks during a test in the summer of 1941 in which ARP services took part. Note the cardboard boxes in which the masks had to be carried wherever one went. Gasmasks for the area were assembled in the former Grange Road Methodist Church, not far from this spot.

The first ARP control in Middlesbrough was established in the disused Unitarian Trinity Church in Corporation Road, but in one of the first air raids, bombs shook the place so much that a purpose-built control centre was erected on education land at Sandy Flatts, just behind the three cottages in Acklam Road, opposite Malvern Drive. It came into operation about December, 1941. After the war the building was used in connection with the school playing fields.

Purpose-built depots for rescue parties were put up in late 1941. There were four: one on land belonging to the Co-operative Society on Acklam Road, near the junction with Green Lane (the premises were later to become a social club); another in Park Road South, adjoining St Joseph's Church (this one, too, was destined to be turned into a social club); a third in Green Lane next to St Mary's Church Hall, later to be used by the police; and the fourth in Cargo Fleet Lane, opposite Brambles Farm Hotel (later let to an ice-cream firm).

St Aidan's Lodge, the vicar's residence which formerly stood in Linthorpe Road where the present Polytechnic hall of residence has been built, was bought by the council in 1938 and equipped for anti-gas training for ARP personnel. Most instructors were school teachers who had volunteered for the task after their own training.

Fireguards, or firewatchers, were organised in the summer of 1941 and reorganised in the autumn of 1943 to give duties in street fire parties and at business premises. "This was a colossal undertaking which involved firstly the enrolment of volunteers and then the organisation of a measure of compulsion for thousands of people," commented one official involved.

Nevertheless, the organisation helped to save many houses and other buildings from serious loss by fire from incendiary bombs.

Any account of wartime activities on the home front must make special mention of that handmaiden of all services, the air raid warden, who assembled and distributed respirators, liaised with all the other services and then found time after nearly three years' action to form the backbone of the 'fireguard'.

Air raid personnel were not immune to the actions of the enemy. Mr Albert Stockwell, who served in the control centre as Mr Preston Kitchen's right-hand man throughout the war, and was later to become town clerk of Thornaby, had his own personal experience of tragedy during the attacks on Middlesbrough. In April, 1942, he visited London to see the capital's Civil Defence force in operation. During one raid he was taken by the city's medical adviser to the top of a high building for a view of the scene. "It was terrifying," he recalled.

Weary and tired after his visit, Mr Stockwell arrived back at his London hotel late at night, but was aroused about 2am to be told that his mother had been killed in an air raid which had destroyed the family home near Newport Bridge. His father died three days later from injuries he received.

The family disaster could have been even worse. "I had a sister," Mr Stockwell explained, "but because I was away in London my wife asked her to stay with her. It saved her life..."

15. Work is well under way on Trinity Church Hall, Middlesbrough, to convert the building into the town's first ARP Control.

16. Members of a Gas Identification Squad. Recruited from the ranks of qualified chemists, their job was to identify the various types of gas which might be dropped by the enemy — lung irritants, blister gases, tear gases etc.

A Fire Officer Remembers

Stan Haggath had been a member of the AFS — a volunteer part-timer — for just a year when World War Two broke out. Automatically he became a full-time firefighter and found himself a section officer in charge of the AFS contingent covering South Bank, Normanby and Teesville in the Eston Urban District, his light trailer pump hitched behind the baker's van of which he had been driver/salesman until 3 September 1939.

He and his men were in action at many of the incidents which occurred over the next few years not only in the South Bank area but also, after being merged into the National Fire Service (NFS) in April 1941, in Middlesbrough. He also had a grim taste of the blitz in Manchester and Liverpool.

Ironically he missed the first raid on his own area, on 25 May 1940, because it happened on a Sunday — and Sunday was his one night off in the week!

Stan remembers the night a German bomber collided with a barrage balloon cable and crashed on to the railway at South Bank: "We had an action station in a former chapel in Lorne Terrace," he recalled. "We heard this plane coming down with its engines going full blast. There was a hell of a crunch — then dead silence. I had dived for cover underneath the table with one of the telephonists. The aircraft had hit the cable of a balloon on the slag tip at Clay Lane and crashed on the railway, between Clay Lane works and the main Saltburn-Middlesbrough line. I attended the blaze; there was a big crater and the plane's crew were all killed." Balls of slag, thrown up by the impact, damaged the roof of his station but all the appliances had been dispersed, as was the practice during an alert, and they escaped damage.

On another occasion an enemy raider was shot down over Eston Hills and came to grief on Barnaby Moor. "The second-in-command of the Eston brigade was Tommy Marks," said Stan. "We saw this dogfight over Eston Hills. I lived at Teesville at the time and immediately went down on my motor-bike to the station at South Bank football ground. Tommy Marks had a car there and we jumped in and went up to Flatts Lane. A group of youths flagged us down near the dense woodland at the bottom of the bank and said a German had parachuted into the woods. We went in and got so far before we realised the German was probably armed — so we carried on a little more cautiously. We found the airman dead in a ditch, still in his parachute harness, which was entangled in trees. The Home Guard were on exercises in the area and Lieutenant Philip Thompson, who was in charge of the local unit, came on the scene, so we passed the body over to him."

In 1942 Stan was among the small army of firefighters who tackled the spectacular blazes at the Binns and Dickson & Benson's stores in Middlesbrough — neither caused by enemy action. "For both of them we relayed water from Middlesbrough Dock," he recalled. "We had static water tanks situated at various strategic points around the town and there was one at the junction of Corporation Road, Marton Road and Bright Street. Water was relayed into this tank from the dock, then pumped through hoses along Corporation Road to the fireground."

Stan's most taxing experiences of the war came at the end of 1940 and the early part of 1941 when the Germans launched their terrifying attacks on major provincial British cities. Fire crews from all over the country were dispatched to help out the beleagured firemen in these target areas and Stan was in charge of a machine which went from Eston to assist at Manchester and Liverpool.

Other reinforcements were sent from Middlesbrough and other parts of the north. The Eston crew met with other fire engines at Darlington early on 23 December 1940, and drove in convoy to Manchester, picking up appliances from other brigades on the way.

"We got more experience in a matter of days than you would get in months or years of peacetime firefighting," he commented. "Up to then I had never seen anything more than chimney fires and house fires — and I was suddenly pitched into a scene of six, ten and twelve-storey buildings, well alight. As fast as you put one out you had to go round the corner and start on another one. On one occasion in Manchester we had to take over from a crew who had all just been killed — with remnants of their gear still lying around. We had to take over their equipment and carry on with the job they had been doing."

Stan continued to serve with the NFS until it was denationalised in 1948 then moved to Middlesbrough, eventually becoming deputy chief officer of the town's brigade.

18. Stan Haggath (*left*) with an AFS car and a Sigmond light trailer pump, pictured outside the Co-op bakery in South Terrace, South Bank, which had been his workplace and, with the outbreak of war, became his first AFS station. Note the sandbagged entrance. This car was the one which took Stan and other Eston auxiliary fireman to Manchester at Christmas, 1940, together with a trailer pump, to assist during the city's three-night blitz. Other firemen in the photograph are *left to right:* T Jameson, A Peacock, N Robinson and S Ainsworth.

19. AFS firefloat on exercise in Middlesbrough, September 1939. When the bombing began in earnest many brigades responsible for areas of dockland were equipped with special shallow-draft fireboats fitted with coffer dams which could suck up water within themselves so as to feed high-pressure deck-mounted water cannon.

22. Wynyard Hall, near Wolviston, served as a training school for No 2 Area of the National Fire Service, which stretched from Scarborough in the south to Bishop Auckland and Barnard Castle in the north. Later the school was move to Scalby Hall. Stan Haggarth became chief instructor at Wynyard and is pictured here in the centre of the front row (with arms folded). This photograph of firemen who took part in a refresher course in January-February, 1944, was taken in front of the hall.

23. The regular members of the Middlesbrough Rescue Service in World War Two. Those seated in the front row include: Borough Engineer, Mr Gorman (dark overcoat) then to the right (light overcoat) Mr Midgeley, Borough Engineer's dept; to the left of Mr Gorman (in uniform with gloves) Mr Oates Lithgow (commandant), Mr Pearse (adjutant, Control Centre); and Mr Beeforth (Rescue Service instructor). Reg Hebden is seated front row fourth from right.

Tradesmen turned Rescuers

The men who dug out the living and the dead from the rubble of Middlesbrough's air raids began learning rescue techniques some eight months before the outbreak of the Second World War.

Most of the eighty-four regulars who first comprised the Rescue Service were building trades employees from the Borough Engineer's Department of Middlesbrough Corporation. Bricklayers, joiners, painters, plumbers, riggers etc attended lectures every Thursday in the board yard in Commercial Street and the officers were chosen from these after exams.

They were thinly spread across ten rescue stations, but the organisers of the service had to think again when demands on the time of the personnel seriously affected the running of the Borough Engineer's Department.

It was then that the pack was reshuffled, with some employees being replaced by employers and employees from local private building firms. They were, in turn, backed up by five hundred volunteers from various manual trades, such as dockers, steelworkers etc. The regulars' shifts were twenty-four hours on duty and twenty-four hours off, supported by the volunteers who were on duty from 7pm to 7am once a week.

Two squads of ten men (a mix of regulars and volunteers) plus a party leader for each and one station officer were on duty all the time. Eventually four purpose-built stations were located in Brambles Farm, Clairville, Green Lane, and Acklam Road. Training included two spells of two weeks at Great Ayton in company with other rescue squads from all over the north resulting in as many as five hundred men being in the camp at one time.

When the war began, the Rescue Service used converted lorries and all suitable equipment to hand. Within a year they boasted purpose-built rescue vehicles with every tool imaginable for tunnelling into debris and removing rubble. Call-out clothing included uniforms, heavy anti-gas suits, helmets, overalls and gasmasks.

Before the sirens warned the local population the Rescue Service was alerted by central control, who telephoned a yellow warning when raiders were approaching and a red alert just before they arrived over a district.

"Which calls you answered depended on which squad you were in," remembers Reginald Hebden. "The first squad was nearly always involved during the air raids, while the second squad generally went out later, often the following day, to look for missing persons in the debris.

"The night we were called to the bombing of Bell Street it was 11.45pm and incendiaries were falling all over the Newport area. We arrived to find the top of one house blazing and three men carrying furniture out into the street. There were huge cracks running down the walls of the house and we could see through to the shop next door. I told the men the place was dangerous and to stop going inside, but they were struggling with a piano and wouldn't take any notice. I had to get a policeman to tell them to stop.

"Through the flames inside I could see a woman carrying bags of sugar out of the shop and we had to stop her. Just then six firemen arrived with an auxiliary pump on the back of a lorry, but when they turned the water on the jet hit an electrical fixture inside and the shock ran back over to knock the men down and stop the pump working any more. They had to send for another.

"I was a member of the second squad when we went to search for missing people in an area just behind Mills Street. Three houses were down in a huge pile of rubble and we were told that a woman was missing. The first squad had searched the night before and found nothing, so I spoke to her husband, an air raid warden, who had just left his home to go on duty when the bomb fell. He said he left his wife still getting dressed in the bedroom before she went into the shelter. This gave me some idea of where she might be buried and I decided to start at the top of the rubble.

"Just by chance a messenger boy had arrived and I asked if he would help by climbing to the top of the mound. It was against regulations to involve a boy of his age, but he was a lightweight and I suggested he removed one brick at a time from the top of the pile. He had only been throwing bricks down for a few minutes when he shouted: 'Mister, will you come up here." When I climbed up I saw a foot sticking out. I told the boy to go and get a cup of tea at the Salvation Army teastall in the street while five of us began to remove the rubble. One of the men got his hands covered in blood, but we were able to check she was dead before lifting her on to a stretcher."

First Aid With A Smile

Few people experienced more of the horrors of the air raids on Middlesbrough than Borough Freeman and former councillor Mrs Ethel Gaunt, who has vivid memories of her four years in a busy first-aid post.

From 1940 to 1944 she saw duty during the raids at the first-aid post established in a Wesleyan chapel in Lower Lord Street, off Newport Road (behind the Cannon Hotel). Spare time was spent helping out at the North Riding Infirmary which was then the principal casualty hospital.

The post was looked after by a team of women members of the Red Cross and the St John Ambulance Brigade, while the men had their headquarters in Holy Cross Church in Lord Street. Mrs Gaunt explained how the men would go out and bring the casualties back on stretchers for the women to tend. "There were some pretty grim sights," she admits. She recalls that the night the Leeds Hotel was demolished by a bomb, all the windows of the first-aid post were blown in and the nurses were unable to put any lights on. So they transferred their operations to the cellar of Holy Cross Church across the road. There they hit a snag. 'When we got the casualties bandaged up — some had shattered limbs — we could not get them out of the cellar on the stretchers."

She remembers walking round the Wilson Street area the following morning to see the damage.

Life had its lighter side. Mrs Gaunt tells of the night rescuers were called to extricate a man trapped in rubble after a bomb had dropped between two street shelters in Marsh Road. "His legs were sticking out and they tried to pull him out by his feet," she said. "But his legs came away. The rescuers nearly died with shock — but it turned out that he had lost both his legs in the First World War and wore two artificial ones!"

Mrs Gaunt well remembers her birthday celebration in October 1940. On the night of Sunday 13 October — three days after her birthday — she had invited her colleagues from both shifts to a small party at the first-aid post.

"We were sitting round the table drinking Green Goddess cocktails when one of the women suddenly said, 'Have you counted? There are thirteen of us — and it is 13 October.'

"Then bombs dropped on Hatherley Street and Benjamin Street and the windows of the post were blown in and everything was covered in dirt and dust, including all the dressings and instruments we had sterilised and prepared for use. Our faces were black, too. Then the casualties started arriving. That was the end of the party."

The Home Front

Life on the Home Front continued against a background of evacuation, blackout, air raids, rationing of food and clothing, together with warden, firewatching and Home Guard duties. Local factories and works toiled flat out to boost the war effort, with women playing a vital role, taking on much of the heavy work formerly done by their menfolk, now in the forces.

Food rationing was introduced in January, 1940. Everyone had a ration book and had to register at a specific shop for each commodity. At that time each person was allowed twelve ounces of sugar, four ounces of butter and four ounces of bacon per week. Later, other items were added to the rationing list, including eggs, cheese, tea, margarine and sweets. From March, 1940, meat was rationed by price. Excluded, however, were offal, poultry, game, sausage and pies. Things like bread, vegetables, fresh fruit, fish and potatoes could be bought when they were available — and queues quickly formed as word got round! A *Dig for Victory* campaign was launched to encourage people to turn their gardens over to vegetables and parkland and other open space was brought into productive use. Housewives found ingenious ways of producing tasty meals with unlikely ingredients as shortages began to bite.

Clothes were rationed from June, 1941, with each person allowed a given number of coupons and each garment carrying a specified coupon value. Again, a good deal of ingenuity was exercised. 'Utility' clothing and bedding became a familiar sight in the shops.

Young women were conscripted into the services or into essential war work. Railings and gates disappeared as the call went out for scrap metal to aid the war effort. Waste paper was collected to be repulped.

At regular intervals during the war, savings drives were launched in each area to raise cash to pay for the war. Street savings groups were formed. There was, in Middlesbrough, a Spitfire Week, a Warships Week, and a Wings for Victory Week. A War Weapons Week in February, 1941, realised £1.16 million — 'the cost of three destroyers" — bringing the town's total savings to date to £3 million. A Salute the Soldier week in May 1944 raised almost the same amount. The destroyer HMS *Cleveland* was adopted by Middlesbrough and in March 1943, the commander exchanged plaques with the mayor. A Battle of Britain drumhead service was held in Albert Park in September, 1943. The following month, the first repatriated prisoners of war arrived home from Germany.

With television not yet in vogue, the 'wireless' and the cinema provided the chief forms of entertainment. Radio programmes like Tommy Handley's incomparable *ITMA* (It's That Man Again), Jack Warner's *Garrison Theatre*, Arthur Askey's *Bandwagon*, *Much Binding in the Marsh* and *Hi Gang* were eagerly anticipated each week — and produced their own crop of catch phrases which became part of everyday exchanges. Some survive to this day. The Empire Theatre, Middlesbrough, helped to keep spirits up with weekly variety shows, featuring such favourites as Wilfred Pickles (billed as "the well-known BBC announcer"), pianist Charlie Kunz, comedian Syd Walker ('radio musical hall star — 'wot would you do chum?' "), mouth organ virtuoso Ronald Chesney, Barry Lupino, those 'cads' the Western Brothers (Kenneth and George), Joe Davis ('the wizard of the cue'), comedian Billy Russell and Felix Mendelssohn's Hawaiian Seranaders.

Unnecessary travel was discouraged, partly to relieve pressure on public transport and also to save fuel. Local Authorities were urged to organise programmes of entertainment during the summer holidays to encourage residents to stay put. A Holidays at Home programme was arranged in Middlesbrough in 1941, centred chiefly on the town's parks.

MINISTRY OF FOOD

REGISTRATION

for

BACON & HAM • BUTTER • SUGAR

All ration books have now been posted, and all members of the public should register with their shopkeepers for Bacon & Ham, Butter and Sugar before

Thursday, 23rd November

Registration is a necessary measure to ensure adequate supplies and fair distribution. It is essential to the smooth working of food distribution in war-time.

— SIMPLE INSTRUCTIONS FOR YOUR GUIDANCE —

1. Put your name and address at the bottom of the Bacon & Ham, Butter and Sugar pages of your Ration Book *NOW*.

2. Write on page II (The inside cover of your Ration Book) the name and address of your shopkeeper for each of the three foods:—Bacon, Butter and Sugar.

3. Take your Ration Book to your shopkeepers for Bacon & Ham, Butter and Sugar.

4. Let the shopkeepers write their names and addresses on the appropriate counterfoils and cut them out.

5. The numbered coupons should not be cut out yet. This will be done by the shopkeepers when rationing begins.

6. Only the pages for Bacon & Ham, Butter and Sugar are to be used. You should *not* register for any other food.

7. Although the page for Butter includes Margarine ignore this, as Margarine is not being rationed.

8. Sugar is not being rationed at present, but registration is necessary.

9. If you change your address, take your Ration Book to the Local Food Officer in your new district.

10. Don't forget that you are free to choose your own shopkeepers.

A SHOPKEEPER WILL ONLY BE ABLE TO GET SUPPLIES FOR HIS REGISTERED CUSTOMERS

REGISTER NOW

AN ANNOUNCEMENT BY THE MINISTRY OF FOOD, GT. WESTMINSTER HOUSE, LONDON, S.W.1

26. *Above:* Middlesbrough's first gasbag car, belonging to the Gas Department, October 1939.

29. Schoolboys help with the harvest.

30. Digging for victory on a site close to Middlesbrough's Cenotaph, in front of the Albert Park, alongside Linthorpe Road. McAdams' Garage can be seen in the background at the corner of Kensington Road. The short length connecting Ayresome Street with Park Road North to form the Cross-town Route was not constructed until some years after the war. The site in the picture is now occupied by public gardens.

Defence Services Inspected

STORIES of devotion to duty during enemy action by a young woman telephonist at the local A.R.P. control centre, and by a senior fireman, were unfolded to the King and Queen when they made an informal visit to Middlesbrough on Thursday for an inspection of the civil defence personnel. →June 19,1941.

Their Majesties' visit had been kept a close secret, and official invitations were not sent out until only a few hours beforehand. Even those who were being inspected did not know who the "important personages" were when they received their notices, and there had been much speculation.

Thousands of people lined the streets and cheered their Majesties and at two or three vantage points, residents stood four to five deep. Shop and office girls on the route leaned from the windows.

As their Majesties crossed the boundary, the King was seen to point out to the Queen a landmark which they opened a few years ago.

Tremendous cheers greeted the King and Queen when they reached the centre of the town and they frequently bowed to acknowledge the greetings of the people.

THE QUEEN talking to Coun. E. Whatley, officer-in-charge of the A.R.P. Control Centre, and Miss E. Crutchley.

32. Royal visit, 19 June 1941. Secrecy surrounded a visit by the King and Queen to Middlesbrough on Thursday, 19 June 1941, when they inspected local Civil Defence personnel in Albert Park. "It was very hush-hush," recalls Albert Stockwell. "Nobody knew who was coming. It was kept very tight." Official invitations were not sent out until just a few hours beforehand. Even those on parade did not know who the 'important personages' were to be. Nevertheless newspaper reports record that thousands of people lined the streets and cheered the Royal couple, and shop and office girls leaned out of upstairs windows to greet them. At the park their Majesties were welcomed by the Mayor and Mayoress, Councillor Sir William and Lady Crosthwaite, the Deputy Mayor (Councillor Tom Meehan), the Town Clerk and Controller (Mr Preston Kitchen) and the Chief Constable (Mr Alfred Edwards).

Among those presented to the Royal visitors was Miss Elizabeth Crutchley, a telephonist in the ARP control, who was on duty during one raid when her family's home in Victoria Road was among a number damaged by HE bombs. She calmly continued taking down messages about the incidents during the raid. She told the Queen her family had all been in the shelter when the attack took place.

35. The latest in utility haute couture? It's May 1942 and models pose for the press. *left:* Short sleeved spring dress in light blue wool with navy contrast. *centre:* Short-sleeved spring dress in navy and white check Scottish tweed. *right:* Summer tunic style dress in brown and white rayon linen.

36. Officially approved wooden soles. The sole and heel were made of birch or poplar and the toe was curved up to allow for the heel-toe action in walking. Leather treads, which had to be renewed before they were too worn, were nailed to the wood. January 1943.

41. Holidays at home. Country dancing, Pallister Park, North Ormesby, Middlesbrough.

2. Holidays at home. Beach amusements and barbed wire at Redcar. Unnecessary travel was discouraged, partly to relieve pressure on public transport and also to save fuel.

43. Redcar beach entrance and pier. The curious looking piece of modern sculpture was in fact part of the local defences. The curved block was intended to be rolled into the gap to delay invading troops from getting off the beach.

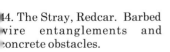

44. The Stray, Redcar. Barbed wire entanglements and concrete obstacles.

Industry

As a major steel, engineering, shipbuilding and chemical centre, Teesside played a vital role in the war effort. Firms large and small made their contribution in an amazing variety of ways.

For instance, in the five years of war (an industrial correspondent recorded afterwards) Dorman Long & Company — later to become part of British Steel — turned out more than 6.5 million tons of ingots, mined more than sixteen million tons of coal, 8.75 tons of ironstone and 1.5 million tons of limestone.

The ironstone mines of Cleveland, which had been running down since the 1920s, came into their own again as foreign ores became difficult to obtain.

From Dorman Long's by-products plants came anthracene for the manufacture of khaki dyes, toluene for explosives and benzine for other war purposes.

One of the largest construction shops in Middlesbrough was laid out and equipped for rapid mass production of highly specialised floating bridgework.

Tees Side Bridge & Engineering Works Ltd, a Dorman Long subsidiary, had an extremely busy war. Apart from air raid shelters, tank turrets, several types of aircraft hangars, armoured car bodies and bridges, the firm produced landing craft, gunboats and rocket-firing craft.

In November, 1940, Tees Side Bridge took over Cleveland dockyard, a disused shipyard on the Tees near Middlesbrough Dock which formerly belonged to Raylton Dixon, and began making tank landing craft.

The vessels, as the late Mr Thomas R Tighe, a former director and chief engineer, wrote in his history of the company years later, were fabricated in the bridgeyard and transported in pieces to the riverside site, where they were assembled and fitted out complete, ready to sail away.

The British craft had a drop ramp in the bows, but some American-type craft had opening doors.

"In addition to tank landing craft, this form of prefabricated construction was used for supporting vessels, gunboats and rocket-firing craft," said Mr Tighe. "Altogether, the yard produced 214 landing craft, thirty gunboats and forty-eight rocket-firing craft...In addition to these 292 vessels, the dockyard built ten salvage vessels, much larger than the fighting craft. These weighed about 500 tons each and were fully equipped to lift 750 tons...working in pairs."

The rocket ships were designed mainly for use in the Far East and were conveyed there on 'piggy-back' ships, or long transports. Many of the landing craft were used in the Normandy landings.

In his book, Mr Tighe recalls one humorous incident which happened as the first landing craft was departing from the dockyard. "The triple screws (propellers) had been mounted to revolve all in the same direction and the vessel, as it sailed away to the cheers of the workforce, described a large circle in the river and returned back like a boomerang to its starting place — an embarrassment which was readily rectified."

Meantime, the forge and machine shop was working non-stop turning out forged links, levers, gear stampings, sprockets, locking plates and other essential items.

Incidentally, in summing up Tees Side Bridge's efforts, Mr Tighe gives a graphic picture of life in industry during the war. "All this unceasing effort was a great strain on the workforce," he wrote. "Overtime and weekend working, became the norm. The blackout, poor lighting and shortages of good food made men tired and overtried. And after work

there was firewatching on the premises, the Home Guard which occupied the younger men, Civil Defence and fire brigade."

Further along the river at Smith's Dock, South Bank, corvettes, frigates and landing craft were being constructed at a rapid rate. In November, 1939, the cargo vessel *Norman Prince* was launched — appropriately with the yard number 1066! — and this was followed by something like seventy vessels, notably Flower Class corvettes, or coastal patrol vessels, all named after flowers.

The *Gladiolus*, completed in five-and-a-half months from the laying of her keel, was the prototype and was based on the design of the *Southern Pride*, a manoeuvrable whalecatcher built by Smith's Dock in 1936. The Flower Class ships were originally intended for service in the North Sea and around the coast. However, as Mr William Harrison, former chief draughtsman, recalled in a history of the firm written in his own hand and now in the County Archives, due to the extreme shortage of convoy escort vessels, they were sent to the North Atlantic and the Western Approaches — "and it soon became apparent that the original design was not suitable for North Atlantic conditions."

Alterations were designed and applied to vessels under construction, while existing corvettes were recalled one by one for modification. The outcome was the Castle Class corvette, longer and with increased bunker capacity giving the ships a much greater range. A further development was the River Class frigate.

The Flower Class vessels proved a valuable workhorse and 259 were built in the United Kingdom and Canada, from plans supplied by Smith's Dock. Nineteen were constructed by Smith's Dock themselves. In all, thirty-three were lost.

Commander Bower, MP for Cleveland, had retired from the Royal Navy but was recalled and given command of a corvette. He went to South Bank to take it over. Mr Harrison wrote: "He was a tall man and the joiners had to make alterations to his bed to suit his height."

His ship was one of those sent to the North Atlantic — and later, questions were asked in Parliament about the ships' suitability, leading to the modifications.

Mr Harrison also recorded that on the day France surrendered in 1940, the French corvette *La Bastiase* was sunk while on sea trials, apparently after hitting a mine. A number of Smith's dock technical staff were lost and this resulted on a ban on the firm's personnel going to sea on trials.

The ban had to be lifted in August 1943, however, to solve a mystery. The frigate *Odzani* went on trials from the Tees but had to return with machinery trouble. The problem, it was thought, was rectified and she was sent out again — only to return once more with the same complaint.

Mr Harrison takes up the story in his notes: "The only way to solve it was for Smith's Dock representatives to go out on trial..." Four men went, including Mr Harrison himself, Admiralty permission having been obtained.

"We left the yard early one morning with an air escort. The full naval complement were on board, the commanding officer being Lieutenant Commander L A Sayers, RNR. The entrance to the Tees was mined and an old merchant ship, *Clarissa Radcliffe*, was an obstruction. The aeroplane overhead followed us through the minefield, his signal lamp winking from time to time. When we were well clear of the Tees mouth the ship headed due North and the speed began to increase."

The search for the source of the trouble went on and

eventually road grit was found in the starboard side shaft bearings. A sample was put into an envelope and later analysed at South Bank.

"It was found that this grit was similar to the grit on the main road leading to the dockyard. Sabotage by some person unknown," concludes Mr Harrison cryptically.

The bearings were cleaned and the ship headed back for the Tees.

As war tactics changed, new ideas were incorporated into the construction of warships. A River Class frigate, HMS *Rother*, completed at South Bank in 1942, liberated Christmas Island, the last British territory to be freed from the Japanese. The last frigate launched at Smith's Dock, one week after D-Day, was the *Loch Eil*.

The penultimate frigate, *Loch Carron*, was renamed *Surprise* and in 1953 acted as stand-in for the Royal yacht at the Coronation Fleet Review.

The dockyard was also kept at full stretch repairing damaged ships. In 1944, Smith's received an order from the Admiralty to fabricate some 'rather big" solid steel tanks. Shipyard workers were puzzled — but in fact the tanks were to form part of the Mulberry Harbour which played such an important part in getting supplies ashore following the invasion of Normandy.

With the end of the war, Smith's Dock had the task of converting armed trawlers, which had done duty as minesweepers, back to fishing vessels, to supplement food supplies.

The Furness Shipbuilding Company, at Haverton Hill, built the prototype of a class of fast merchant ship capable of beating the U-boat menace by being fast enough to sail independently of convoys. They were claimed to be completely successful; the first one was the *Empire Chieftain*. She survived the war.

Also from Furness came tankers ranging from 400 to 14,000 tons, as well as escort ships and two salvage vessels, each with a lifting capacity of 1,500 tons.

The conversion of a liner, completion of a fleet of small craft for D-Day and the laying-out of design and working plans for landing craft built on the Tees were among other wartime jobs undertaken at Haverton Hill.

Head Wrightson & Company, the engineering firm, worked flat out producing landing craft, bombs of all sizes, armoured cars and sea mines. They were also involved in the development of PLUTO (the pipe line under the ocean), which was uncoiled across the Channel so that fuel could be pumped to our invasion forces after D-Day. And, in co-operation with Ashmore, Benson, Pease, the firm manufactured sections of the Mulberry Harbour.

Aviation fuel, Perspex for aircraft cockpit covers and ammonia for explosives and fertilisers (essential for the *Dig for Victory* campaign) were among the products turned out by ICI Billingham to aid the war effort. But it also had a hand in the development of the atom bomb and, surprisingly, an anti-tank weapon.

45. *Wardens' Post*, the official journal of Middlesbrough's air raid wardens, jokingly described the blackout as "a state of darkness especially designed to aid courting, cause pedestrians to walk into lampposts, pillar boxes and other people, and increase the sale of white paint and black cloth." Local works had special blackout problems. Councillor Bill Herlingshaw explained the measures taken at the coke ovens at Cleveland Works, Grangetown. "Red hot coke had to be pushed out from the ovens," he said, "and that had to be boxed in. This made it a terrible job for the men. They sheeted it all to make a big shed over it so that when they pushed the ovens out through the guide and into the coke car, it was all enclosed to prevent a glare being created which might have attracted enemy bombers. The heat and the fumes inside there were terrible." As a footnote, he recalled how a battery of anti-aircraft rocket guns stationed in a field behind Cleveland House, the Eston Urban Council offices close to the works, opened fire on a German raider one night and shot a piece out of the 320-foot high smoke stack serving the South Battery of coke ovens!
Records in the British Steel archives reveal some of the measures taken to hide flames and glare at the Acklam and Britannia Works in Middlesbrough. To enable slag to be transferred during the hours of darkness from the various parts of the works to the disposal plant, ladles were fitted with lids and lifting gear installed at the furnaces and at the disposal site to raise and lower them. In this picture, over ten tons of molten steel at 1650 degrees centigrade is poured into a ladle.

Before the war, Billingham boasted the only ammonia factory in the country — and, as such, would have been an obvious target for enemy bombers. So in 1938 plans were made to build ammonia plants in areas less vulnerable. They were operated by ICI Billingham but owned by the Ministry of Supply.

Equally important, in 1941 a factory for the vital catalysts was set up in the relative safety of Clitheroe, Lancashire. The first catalyst to be made there was one that enabled high octane fuel to be produced so that Spitfires could fly fast enough to catch the German 'Doodlebugs' — the V1 flying bombs.

In July, 1944, Sir Stafford Cripps, Minister of Aircraft Production, wrote to Billingham thanking the firm and its workers for its output of aviation fuel and urging 'the utmost effort" needed in the coming months to produce the greatest possible quantity.

It was not only ICI's chemical expertise which contributed to the war effort. In April 1942 the engineering department at Billingham was commissioned to design the PIAT gun (Protector, Infantry, Anti-Tank). By November 1943, 100,000 had been built and supplied. Six Victoria Crosses were won by soldiers using the weapon.

In a booklet written by Julian Phillips, former intelligence manager, ICI's part in the development of the atom bomb is outlined. It was known as Operation Tube Alloys. Before the war Billingham had been working on the vital heavy water (deuterium oxide D2O) and the then chairman of ICI, Lord McGowan, was anxious that ICI should lead the team under the research director, Dr Akers.

"However, it became evident early on that the necessary uranium gaseous diffusion plant would stretch all the way from Billingham to Durham, and not even a smokescreen could hide that! So it was not surprising that, when the USA entered the war, the combined effort should move to the safety and secure isolation of the Nevada desert."

The Stockton joinery firm of F Hills & Son Ltd played an unusual but important role.

In 1937 the company had built an aeronautical plywood factory at Manchester and had begun to produce Jablo propeller blades and the successful Praga light aeroplane.

Ironically, the Jablo blade, made from highly compressed wood to give added strength, had been invented by a German and developed by a German firm, Heine. Hills took on their manufacture in this country under licence before the war so the Manchester factory was already equipped to produce them. During the war, the Stockton factory also made the propellers, as well as aeronautical plywood, in very thin sections usually less than one millimetre in thickness, which was used for the 'stressed-skin' construction of the Mosquito fighter and for the wings of the Avro Anson and the Airspeed Oxford trainer.

The Manchester establishment was turning out propellers and also aircraft (the Proctor and the Anson).

Hills took over Terry's chocolate factory at York about 1942 to make propeller blades — used on Spitfires, Hurricanes and a variety of other fighters and bombers.

Meanwhile, in a small workshop off Boathouse Lane, Stockton, strips of paper-backed aluminium foil were being produced, to be dropped by Allied planes to confuse enemy radar. In all, Hills made a total of 480,000 Jablo blades, 812 Percival Proctor aircraft, over ten million square feet of aeronautical plywood (six million of which went into the construction of the Mosquito) and 13,500 trailing edges for Anson wings.

At the peak of the war, twenty-six separate organisations were functioning under Hills' management.

Mr Jim Ellison, formerly technical manager of Hills, who was involved in the operation at both Stockton and Manchester and visited Germany before the war to study the Heine manufacturing methods, recalls that Dorman Long in Middlesbrough possessed the only testing machine which could be used to test the propeller blade roots, which had to 'pull' a load of one hundred tons. It was the same machine which had been used to test the links for the Sydney Harbour Bridge.

Richard Hill & Co, of Middlesbrough, turned out Maxweld-welded, criss-cross steel matting which was ordered in large amounts by the Air Ministry for laying down as emergency airstrips. It proved particularly valuable during the advance into Europe after D-Day.

Lionweld, not far from Hills at Newport, made steel flooring and stairtreads for government contracts, as well as Bailey Bridge parts and engine slings and engine stands for the De Havilland aircraft factory. Firms of all sizes made their contributions to winning the war. The Middlesbrough firm of R W Rundle & Co Ltd installed extra equipment to help produce millions of mild steel washers which did duty in many parts of the world and went into the construction of the Mulberry Harbour. The workforce was mostly women.

Gerald Fleming, better known as a garage firm, turned out seven million shells or bomb parts at their Trunk Road factory, thanks to the efforts of 260 women operators and about ten men. Imeson & Finch Ltd, a Stockton engineering company, changed over from peacetime production of mechanical and electrical equipment to the manufacture of bomb components. They were claimed to be the first people to make 1000-lb bomb containers and for some months were the sole manufacturers in this country.

Women played a major part in the industrial war effort, taking over many of the often heavy jobs previously carried out by men in works and factories and even on the docks.

46. *Left* An eighty ton ingot is withdrawn from a furnace.

47-49. *above:* Air raid shelter being 'tested' by staff of Tees Side Bridge & Engineering. *below:* Another type of air raid shelter built by Tees Side Bridge & Engineering.
left: News item, April 1939.

All photos on this page are British Steel plc NRRC copyright.

. A woman welder at the West Hartlepool Works. As in the Great
ar, women once again took over many jobs formerly done by men.
ngle women in the 19-24 age group were called up and given the
oice between the women's services, Civil Defence, and civilian jobs
nsidered essential to the war effort. By the end of the war 500,000
men were serving in the armed forces; at least 260,000 were working
the munitions industry and 770,000 in engineering and vehicle
ilding. Women's wages rose more than men's and in some trades
ere was a move towards equal pay, but in engineering, the average
oman's pay was only half that of her male counterpart.

52. Tees Side Bridge & Engineering built tank landing craft *TLC47*. The tank deck was closed by doors at the fore end but the only overhead protection provided was from tarpaulins spread over steel bar supports. The accommodation and engine room were aft as was the armoured wheelhouse over which was placed an open bridge. Abaft the bridge the deck was extended to the side to accommodate a light AA gun on each wing.

53. *LCT713* built at the Cleveland Dockyard by Tees Side Bridge & Engineering is moored alongside a heavy lift ship en-route to the Far East. Many of *LCT713's* sisters were strengthened to make the passage to the Far East under their own steam. In spite of their relatively flimsy construction they were able to withstand considerable punishment and stress and one of them, after a particularly stormy passsage, entered harbour towing its own disintegrated bow section astern. *LCT2270* was built by Missouri Valley Bridge & Iron Co.

54. The crew of a Tees Side Bridge & Engineering-built support landing craft take an early bath. This type of vessel was introduced to engage the fixed shore defences expected to be encountered in coastal areas suitable for amphibious landings. The incident pictured here occurred in November 1944 at Walcheren, when the vessel was given the task of drawing gunfire from shore batteries whilst the Royal Marines landed at Westkapelle. All photographs on this page are British Steel plc NRRC copyright.

55. *left:* A steady stream of damaged ships arrived at Smith's Dock's South Bank for repair, stretching the yard's versatility to the limit. This was the *Javelin*, a J Class destroyer which was towed into the Tees with collision damage. Extensive repairs were carried out, including the renewal of shell, decks, bulkheads and longitudinals — and complete overhaul of machinery.

56. *below*: *Halcyon*, an Admiralty Minesweeper, which had completed an extensive overhaul and refit at No 12 dry dock (S Bank). On proceeding to sea she was mined off Tees Bay and towed back to S Dock dry docks with her back broken abaft the engine room. The aft end of the vessel had dropped so far below line of keel that it was impossible to clear the dock sill when dry-docking and a Camel (lifting craft) had to be used to raise the abaft end to clear the sill. The vessel was completely renewed abaft the engine room bulkhead, shafting and propellors were completely renewed and engines and auxiliary machinery were removed, overhauled and refitted.

57. Flower class corvette HMS *Sunflower*, launched at Smith's Dock on 19 August 1940 and scrapped at Hayle in August 1947.

58. Flower class corvette HMS *Samphire*, launched at Smith's Dock on 14 April 1941 and lost on 30 January 1943.
59. *below:* Castle class frigate HMS *Kenilworth Castle*, launched in August 1943, scrapped at Llanelly in June 1959.

60. HMS *Towy*. River Class Frigate.

Vessels completed on River Tees during World War Two

	Smith's Dock Co Ltd	Furness Shipbuilding Co Ltd	Stockton Construction Co *	Tees-Side Bridge & Engineering Co
NAVAL				
Corvette	27	-	-	-
Frigate	20	-	-	-
Sloop	-	2	-	-
Minelayer	-	1	-	-
Coastal Salvage Vessel	5	-	-	-
Minesweeping Trawler	15	-	-	-
Tank Landing Craft (LCT)	6	4	218	31
Gun Landing Craft (LCG)	-	-	17	3
Flak Landing Craft (LCF)	-	-	3	4
Rocket Landing Craft (LCS(R))	-	-	5	2
Tank Landing Ship (LST)	2	-	-	-
Tanker	-	5	-	-
Wreck Lifting Lighter	-	2	-	-
MERCHANT				
Dry Cargo	5	9	-	-
Tanker	-	38	-	-
Total at each yard	80	61	243	40
TOTAL	424			

* Consortium of Cleveland Bridge & Engineering Co, Head Wrightson & Co, South Durham Steel & Iron Co Ltd and Whessoe Ltd

Table compiled by Mr John Proud, chairman of the Teesside branch of the World Ship Society

61/62. Visit by Winston Churchill to the Furness Shipbuilding Co.

63. Two of the concrete caissons, code-named Phoenix and used in the construction of the Mulberry Harbour, were built at the Graythorp dry dock of William Gray. This photograph shows the tugs Acklam Cross, NER No 6 and Cleveland maneouvering the first of the caissons out of the dry dock in 1944. Subsequently the caissons were towed south to their assembly point by ocean-going Royal Navy and Dutch tugs. During the early part of the war, three of the Tees Towing Company's fleet of tugs were requisitioned by the Ministry of Shipping, two of them not returning to the Tees till 1946. The Euston Cross and Charing Cross joined the Normandy Invasion armada in 1944. Throughout the war, tugs on the Tees were kept busy dealing with an amazing variety of ships, including vessels of the Royal and Allied Navies.

65. "Take cover, gas!" The Head Wrightson ARP team take a break from a drill session. Many factories had ARP teams, including first aid parties; gas identification squads; auxiliary fire service units; wardens; and rescue squads.

A FEW CARELESS WORDS MAY END IN THIS—

Many lives were lost in the last war through careless talk
Be on your guard! Don't discuss movements of ships or troops

66. ICI Billingham in the 1930s.

A thick blanket of smoke helped to hide the huge ICI works at Billingham from the prying eyes of enemy air crews on many nights during the war. It was created by a convoy of specially-equipped army lorries which lined up near the site and belched out the smelly protective cover.

The operation was recalled later by Cleveland's Deputy County Librarian, Leslie Still: "I lived at Billingham," he explained. "The lorries were manned by the King's Own Scottish Borderers and were normally strung out along the road between Billingham and the Tees Newport Bridge because the prevailing wind was westerly. If the wind changed they sometimes took up position along the Haverton Hill Road.

There was a combustion chamber on the back of the lorry which burned a mixture of oil and water. It was very effective, producing enormous clouds of smoke, but the smell was appalling and there was a lot of oily soot flying about. The two-man crews had to stay there all night to keep them going."

Civil Defence, by T H O'Brien, one of a series of books published by HMSO on the history of World War Two, states that during 1941 and the early part of 1942 a national system of operational control of smoke screens was established, a school was created to train smoke screen operatives and an organisation was formed to manage a fleet of some 1,500 motor vehicles.

"The War Cabinet had authorised the use of Haslar generators (which consumed fuel oil and water at the rates of about 85 and 70 gallons per hour respectively and burned for eight to nine hours) on a large scale. By the end of 1943 these operations were employing some 500 civilians and over 10,000 members of the army. The eight or so smoke screens of July 1940 had grown to over thirty, covering groups of vital points in such places as Birmingham and Coventry.

"In March 1943 the Ministry's responsibility in this sphere was transferred to the War Office and the Air Ministry. The Ministry was then able to claim that none of the establishments protected by smoke screens under its control — for example at Billingham, Derby, Newcastle and Nottingham — though the object of some attention from the enemy, had suffered any important damage..."

In fact, ICI's own records show that between 19 June 1940, and 26 July 1942, a total of ninety-three bombs fell at various points within their Billingham site during eleven raids, but surprisingly little serious damage was caused. However, two soldiers sheltering under a wagon south of the Billingham Beck reservoir were killed in the first raid, on the night of 19-20 June 1940, and another military casualty suffered from "dust in his eyes" during the same raid.

Two parachute mines, on 15-16 April 1941, seriously damaged a silo end together with a distillation plant, maintenance building and gantries at the oil works.

The busiest time for firefighters at the works came on two successive nights in July, 1942. Seventeen fires were dealt with in fifty-two minutes on the night of the 6-7, and twelve fires in forty-six minutes the following night. ICI employees co-operated closely with National Fire Service personnel in tackling the outbreaks.

According to the firm's records, in the second of these raids, "fairly extensive damage" was caused at the butane painting station and products fire station and "serious damage" to tanks at the oil works, together with a "fair amount of damage" at Billingham Reach Wharf.

In the final raid, on the night of 25-26 July 1942, the finished product conveyor annexe at the fertilizer granulating plant was "completely destroyed" and most of the pumps at number four unit pump house at the nitric acid plant were lost. The coal offloading plant and kiln foundations also suffered "considerable damage", while Casebourne's offices were hit by blast. At various times the Synthonia Club, boys' club and cricket field suffered — and four houses south-east of the main offices were seriously damaged in a raid on 6-7 July 1942.

David Bayliss of Thornaby, then an instrument artificer at ICI Billingham, recalled some of the wartime attacks and their consequences:

"In one raid, a pipe bridge in Nitrate Avenue carrying nitrogen, steam and other materials was blasted, causing a shut down of the factory. But engineers carried out improvised repairs and had links restored within a week.

"On another occasion I remember being on night shift and we went into the shelters when the sirens sounded, emerging later to find thousands of fire bombs, about eighteen inches long, all over the roadways. I saw at least six massive dumper trucks stacked full of fire bombs as the clear-up went on. Many of them had not gone off, others had just burned themselves out.

"Another time a very clever German pilot attacked Bamlett's Billingham Reach Wharf where all the tanks were, shot up all the pipelines, then plonked bombs in all the oil tanks. Firemen smothered the lot in foam and let the tanks burn for the rest of the week."

Mr Bayliss had his own busiest time after a landmine came down behind the refinery, knocking out all the instrument panels for the refinery and damaging the refractory columns. "It was about a month before production was restored," he said.

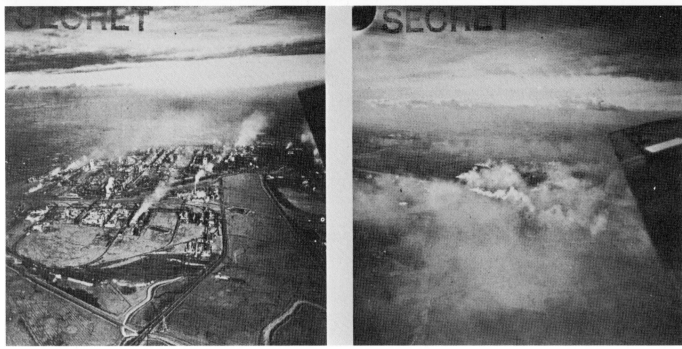

67. ICI Billingham. The picture on the right shows a trial in October 1940 of the smoke screen protecting the works. However, white industrial steam still shows above the screen. To get round this particular problem, pitch was burnt and the black fumes given off were added to the white smoke and resulted in a very effective screening of the site.

68. A Thompson Haslar smoke unit on test.

69. F Hills & Sons, Stockton Works. Making Jablo propellers. Veneer sheets are being fed into the Dryad drying machine — one of the stages in manufacture.

70. Hand finishing the blade contour after shaping.

71. A strange looking Hurricane. A Hurricane was loaned to Hills so that trials could be carried out using a slip wing (the top one), to enable the plane to take off carrying a large bomb slung underneath. Once airborne, the slip wing was released and fell away.

72. A Hillson Praga light plane, produced by Hill at their Manchester factory. A Praga won the Isle of Man 'Round the Island' race and was subsequently flown down to Capetown — both considerable achievements for a light plane of that period.

73. Another Teesside contribution to the war effort was the 'T' type hanger supplied by Tees Side Bridge & Engineering to both the Air Ministry and the Admiralty. *British Steel plc NRRC copyright*

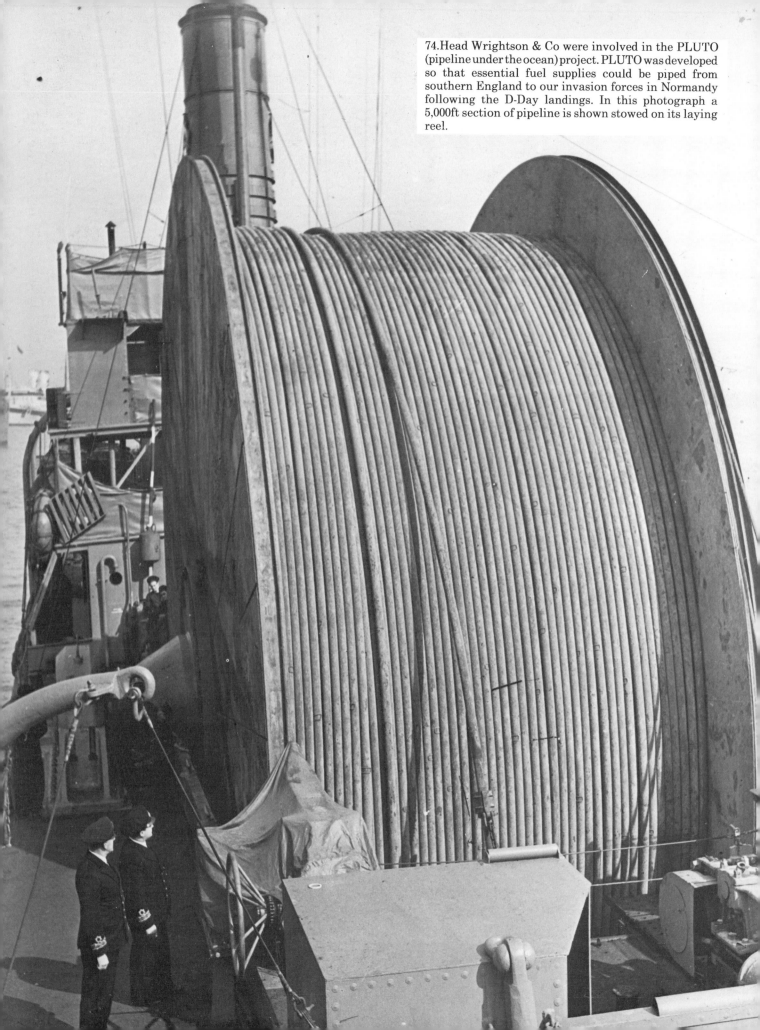

74. Head Wrightson & Co were involved in the PLUTO (pipeline under the ocean) project. PLUTO was developed so that essential fuel supplies could be piped from southern England to our invasion forces in Normandy following the D-Day landings. In this photograph a 5,000ft section of pipeline is shown stowed on its laying reel.

75-76. *above*: Electronically welding the cases of moored mines. *below*: The other side of the coin! Putting the finishing touches to paravanes to give safer passage to British ships through sealanes thought to be mined by the enemy.

Power-Gas Corporation Ltd, of Stockton, was one of the firms responsible for co-ordinating the construction of the famous Mulberry Harbour. Other war work undertaken included: the co-ordination of production by other manufacturers of components for the Bailey Bridge; the construction of complete factories for the production of hydrogen for the RAF balloon barrage; the building of hundreds of producer gas plants providing emergency fuel resources for factories on direct munitions and other wartime necessities; the manufacture and erection of industrial plants such as the gas-fired dolomite calcinating plant used in the manufacture of magnesium; and the dismantling, removal, reconstruction and modernisation of a complete mineral oil refinery.

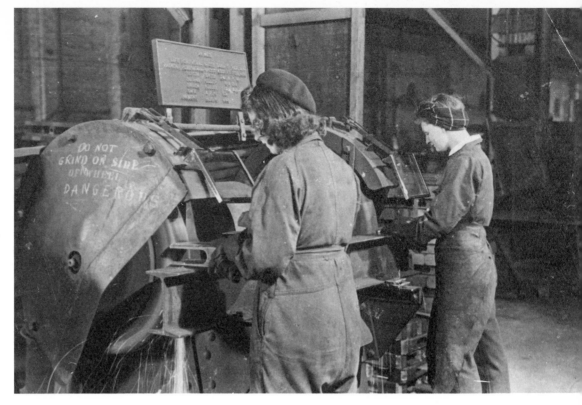

77-78. Women carry out essential war work in the Fitting Shop at Power-Gas Corporation Ltd, of Stockton.

79-80. *above:* A Power-Gas Coroporation firefighting team in practice.
below: As a precaution, several departments of the Power-Gas Corporation were moved from Parkfield Works, Stockton, to the more spacious and elegant setting of Preston Hall.

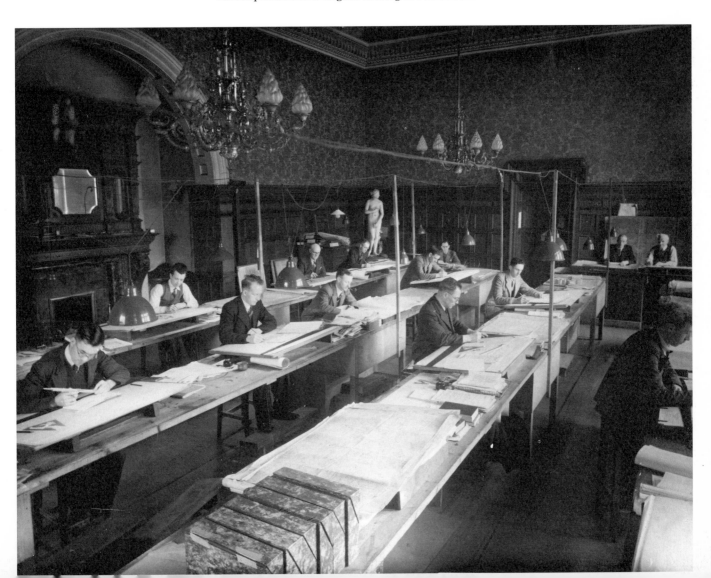

81 Home Guard parade at Preston Hall of units drawn from men working for the Power-Gas Corporation, Stockton and neighbouring factories.

The Home Guard

Yarm platoon of the Home Guard was not, perhaps, typical of the Home Guard in Teesside. Unlike their colleagues, its members, many of them drawn from farms in the area, did not man anti-aircraft batteries, with great efficiency, in industrial Teesside. Nor were they called in to help clear up after bomb attacks.

In fact, this rustically-inclined unit epitomised the 'Dad's Army' spirit, according to John Holt, pharmacist and principal of Strickland & Holt, the well-known Yarm shop, who was quartermaster of the unit. "We had great fun and games," he admitted. "It was a very autocratic outfit! When we started, all we had was a little arm band saying LDV (Local Defence Volunteers). Then gradually supplies began to come through and we got uniforms, boots, helmets and so on. We used to drill with broom shanks before we received any weapons, although a lot of the lads from the country had their own guns — including twelve-bores."

Major Kenneth Evans, from Worsall Hall, a retired army officer, became the first Commanding Officer. He was later succeeded by Major Dickinson, who managed a brass foundry at Stockton. The first consignment of weapons — old Ross Canadian rifles — arrived at Worsall Hall. Mr Holt recalls: "They were packed in barrels of tallow, all greased up, and we had to take them home and clean them. There was a big warehouse, belonging to a coal dealer and haulier, behind where Hinton's store was later developed, and we took over the first floor as our headquarters. We had it full of high explosives — crates of ammunition, stick bombs, grenades and weapons." The platoon's main contribution to the war effort was to ensure the safety of the 43-arch railway viaduct which crosses the town. Using a small platelayers' hut, equipped with uncomfortable bunks, as a base, the Home Guards mounted nightly patrols along the lofty viaduct.

This duty might appear mundane, but it was not without its hazards, as Mr Holt pointed out. "When two trains passed on the viaduct, it was hair-raising. There was scarcely any space left at the side and some of our chaps would actually sit with their legs hanging over the parapet while the trains went past!"

When a German plane was shot down one night and crashed on the field where the Kebbell estate now stands, the Home Guards on duty at the hut just above the cemetery gates dashed to the scene, arriving just as the wreckage burst into flames and ammunition started exploding. "By the time I got there they were all trying desperately to find some cover," says Mr Holt. Some of the incidents involving the unit would have done justice to Captain Mainwaring and his lads in the television series. For instance, there was the soldier who was on duty on the viaduct one night when he spotted a light showing from the rear window of a house below — a serious matter during the blackout. He took the somewhat precipitate and unorthodox action of aiming a shot through the window. No complaint was ever received.

Then there was the occasion when the unit was due to be inspected by a 'brass hat' from Catterick. With boots and brasses highly polished and battledresses smartly creased, the platoon waited expectantly in the Hight Street. As the appointed time came and went, however, there were signs of restlessness in the ranks and when the nearby Black Bull opened its doors all the troops disappeared inside.

While they were sipping their pints, they saw through the window the VIP's car, staff flag and all, passing along the High Street vainly looking for the parade. "We didn't dare show our faces," comments Mr Holt.

During a joint exercise near Northallerton, the Yarm Home Guard crept up on a village to take a strategic point and stealthily made their way through the orchard at the rear of the local pub. "By the time we got through there were no apples left in the poor chap's orchard," recalls Mr Holt.

A trial of a newly-acquired Blacker Bombard mortar

82. Yarm Home Guard. Jack Holt is in the front row, third from right.

produced an amusing incident. The weapon was set up in The Friarage grounds, aimed across the river towards woods in Almond's Bottoms which a scouting party was supposed to have cleared in advance, as it was not known exactly how the mortar would perform. The mortar bomb did not contain any explosive charge.

The order was given to fire and the bomb landed right in the middle of the wood. Over the field telephone Jack Holt heard the voice of Lieutenant Bernard Gogg reporting: "You flushed a couple out." A perplexed and flustered pair of young lovers shot out from among the trees. There was one tragedy during the life of the unit. During one of many fetes held in the Friarage grounds to raise money for various war efforts, the Home Guard fixed up a bo'swain's chair across the Tees. Unfortunately, a boy from the town standing watching the operation got his feet entangled in the rope and was pulled into the river. He drowned despite frantic rescue efforts. In the event of an invasion, the platoon had a scheme ready to blow up the culvert carrying the stream from the pond of Bentley House underneath the main road and into the gully alongside the skinyard. But there was apparently no secret plan to blow up the strategically important Yarm Bridge. "I don't think it was ever suggested," muses Mr Holt. "And we thought too much of the bridge to want to destroy it."

From the *Evening Gazette* of 17 May, 1943:
"Impressive Home Guard parades took place in the Teesside area yesterday to mark the third birthday of the formation of the force. Drumhead services were held at Middlesbrough and Stockton. In Middlesbrough nearly 2,000 members of the 8th and 9th Battalions and of anti-aircraft batteries were present at the service in Albert Park.....More than 1,000 officers and men of the 19th Durham (Stockton) Battalion and anti-aircraft batteries were inspected in Ropner Park..."
And of 1 December, 1944:
"Teesside Home Guards had their final parades yesterday. Thousands of men attended the stand-down ceremonies and big parades took place at Middlesbrough, Stockton and Redcar."

84. Head Wrightson's Home Guard unit.

85-86. Home Guard versus Airborne troops. These pictures were taken by Lieutenant O'Brien on 25 October 1943 during an exercise in the Northern Command when the Home Guard acted the part of defenders of vulnerable points in the Middlesbrough and Stockton-on-Tees area. The assault force consisted of Airborne troops, some of whom had marched sixty-six miles in two days and went straight into action. *above:* Airborne troops in action at Stockton. *left:* After the exercise there was a march past in Middlesbrough. This picture was taken in miserable weather at the intersection of Albert Road and Corporation Road (Town Hall corner). Hintons grocery store stands on the far corner.

87-89. It is not certain who was most startled — German pilots or Teessiders themselves — when a new British rocket-gun, an important anti-aircraft device, was used for the first time in the area in July 1942. Its projectile rocketed into the sky with a terrific rushing noise, described as 'like an express train', bursting with vivid red flashes. In a German broadcast at the time, a Nazi airman said he had just taken part in a raid on Middlesbrough. "The British AA defences were known to be very strong," he was quoted as saying, "but this time they were reinforced by what we German fliers call 'the pilots' terror' — the latest British AA shells. They look like a flaming shell which explodes high in the sky and falls down on our planes in numerous little shells. The whole thing looks like a firework..."

90-91. *Above:* Northern Command heavy anti-aircraft goes into action on a rain-soaked morning in February 1940.
Below: The range-finder and the predictor.

The Bombing

Teesside had the dubious distinction of being the first industrial area in Britain to be attacked by German aircraft.

It happened in the early hours of 25 May 1940, when five bombs were dropped on Cargo Fleet and seven at South Bank and Grangetown. Most fell harmlessly on open space, although one bomb hit the roof of the constructional department at Cargo Fleet Works, the plant itself escaping damage. The only casualties were eight men sitting in a weigh cabin at Dorman Long's South Works steel plant at Grangetown, twenty feet from where one of the bombs exploded. Three were taken to hospital.

The worst havoc was caused at South Bank, where a bomb fell at the rear of Aire Street, causing extensive damage to five houses and their outbuildings. Many people had narrow escapes; one ten-year-old girl was found by her family still fast asleep although her bed was covered in broken glass and splintered woodwork.

No air raid warning was sounded before the bombs fell — a fact which sparked off angry questions among local people. They also complained that ground defences did not go into action, although the plane had been heard for some time circling overhead. The whole incident was over in ten minutes and people had little chance to make for the shelters. The intruder was finally driven off by RAF fighters.

92. South Bank, May 1940.

93. Volunteers man a Royal Observer Corps post in the North-east. They were responsible for tracking enemy raiders and friendly planes alike. In the area bounded by Hartlepool, Scarborough, York and Sedbergh there were forty-one posts, and in the Teesside and Cleveland area they were situated at Eaglescliffe; Eston; Redcar; Seaton Carew; West Hartlepool; Loftus; Saltburn; Hinderwell; Castleton; Ayton; Newton Bewley; Osmotherley and Croft.

94. South Bank football ground after the raid of 25 May 1940. The bomb dropped almost on the penalty spot but the ground survived

95. Four-year-old Richard Walkington standing on the window sill of his bomb-blast damaged home, South Bank.

96. *Luftwaffe* reconnaissance photograph dated 31 August 1939.

In the early hours of Thursday, 27 June 1940, a stick of bombs, dropped by a lone raider, fell in a line from the Transporter Bridge to Middlesbrough Town Hall — but although many thousands of pounds worth of damage was caused, no-one was seriously hurt.

The devastation began at the Anderston Foundry, at the north end of the Transporter. A second bomb missed the superstructure of the bridge, but severed two electricity cables running across the top — and passed through the floor of the Transporter's suspended car, which was standing on the Middlesbrough side of the river, smashing windows and denting steelwork. The bridge was out of action for only a few hours. A short distance to the south a bomb fell in the yard of the Middlesbrough Corporation gasworks. The purifier house was struck and the oxide elevator demolished.

Next, St Peter's Church and vicarage were wrecked, together with the adjoining warehouse of Hambro Supplies Limited in the old Oxford Theatre, Lower Feversham Street. A railway signal box near Dock Street was wiped out.

On the town side of the railway tracks, cottages in Wood Street and School Croft were damaged beyond repair and the rear of the GPO and other business premises suffered.

Destruction was most apparent, however, at the junction of Corporation Road and Albert Road — the Town Hall corner. There, a bomb plummeted into the public conveniences immediately beneath the clock tower, disfiguring all four faces of the clock itself and shattering windows over a wide area. Policemen waiting in the Town Hall Crypt for emergency duty did not need to be told "that was a close one!" The vicar of St Peter's was out on duty as an air raid warden when his church and home were blasted. His wife and six-year-old daughter, who would normally have taken refuge in the cellar of the vicarage, had left two days earlier for a five-day holiday.

WHEN THE SIRENS GO

A notice broadcast yesterday by the Lord Privy Seal's Office said:—

IN the event of threatened air raids, warnings will be given in urban areas by sirens or hooters, which will be sounded in some places by short intermittent blasts and in other places by a warbling note changing every few seconds.

The warning may also be given by short blasts on police whistles. No hooter or siren may be sounded except on the instructions of the police.

When you hear any of these sounds— TAKE SHELTER.

And do not leave your shelter until you hear the "Raiders Passed" signal, which will be given by continuously sounding the sirens or hooters for two minutes on the same note.

98-99. St Peter's Church, Middlesbrough, after the raid of 27 June 1940.

100. A rescue squad at work.

101-102. This shattered council house (*below*) in Meadowfield Avenue, Grove Hill, was the scene of Middlesbrough's first death from enemy action, early on 28 August 1940. The victim was the wife of an air raid warden. She was killed as she was carrying her year-old baby downstairs to shelter. The baby, together with two other children who were in the back scullery at the time, survived. The bomb crater can be seen in the foreground.

Nineteen other people were injured in the attack, in which five HE bombs fell on the area. An emergency feeding centre was opened at Marton Grove School. The house pictured *right*, further along Meadowfield Avenue from where the fatality occurred, also received a direct hit — but three wardens sheltering in the alleyway on the left were unhurt. Blast could play peculiar tricks; one house nearby had all its windows blown out, but sections of a greenhouse, propped up against the wall awaiting assembly, were undamaged. The same night, Grangetown was pasted with fifteen bombs, four of which failed to explode. Homes were wrecked and casualties caused.

103-105. Sunday evening of 13 October 1940 was bright and moonlit and large numbers of people were about in the streets of Middlesbrough as the sirens wailed just after 7.30 pm.

Few of the pedestrians bothered to seek shelter, however — and even after the bombs began to fall on the Newport area with devastating effect at five minutes to eight, Newport Road and Linthorpe Road were still 'thronged with pedestrians,'' Chief Constable Alfred Edwards reported afterwards. Indeed, "the work of the (rescue) services was interfered with by the many sightseers and the position was aggravated when the public houses closed at 10 pm,'' he added.

There is little doubt that the four HE bombs dropped, in what was Middlesbrough's worst incident to date, were intended for nearby industrial plants, particularly Dorman Long & Co's Britannia Works, and the railway sidings.

Industrial targets escaped, however, while severe damage was inflicted on the terraced housing in the Marsh Road-Argyle Street area. Twenty-one people were killed, more than thirty seriously injured and seventy-two slightly hurt. Over 520 people had to be rehoused and about five hundred properties needed repair.

Some of the fatalities occurred in communal shelters which received virtually direct hits. One bomb fell between two of these cast-iron, tubular-type shelters on common land at the junction of Farrer Street and Marsh Road. A huge crater, twelve feet deep and twenty-five feet across, was created, the ends of the shelters were blown out and every house close by in Marsh Road and Argyle Street was demolished. A number of people were killed by this explosion, some of them in the shelter nearest the crater. The boxing stadium in Farrer Street (*centre picture*) was partly demolished.

Another bomb struck the end of a communal shelter on land at the corner of Benjamin Street and Hatherley Street. Only a small crater resulted but considerable damage was caused to houses in the area, particularly in Hatherley Street, and a number of families had to be evacuated.

A third bomb landed in the backs of Benjamin Street and Farrer Street, again resulting in widespread havoc to housing and some fatal casualties.

Only one stick of bombs actually hit an industrial area; it fell on railway premises in the North Road-Metz Bridge area, damaging the LNER goodsmaster's office and blocking North Road. There was slight damage at Britannia Works, Richard Hill & Co's and Lane's brass foundry — and to a refreshment cabin in Forty Foot Road.

In his subsequent report, the chief constable mentioned that fire broke out in twenty-nine houses because fires burning in the grate were blown out into living rooms.

One woman who had arrived from London only the previous day and was staying with her sister while waiting for her furniture to arrive, told the *Gazette* she was at the window getting washed when she was blown under the kitchen table. Luckily she suffered only bruising. But the house she was to have prepared for herself was demolished. Rescue workers who dug feverishly at the debris of one of the partially collapsed shelters found a man protecting a baby under his body — but both were dead. One mother and her three children in one of the shattered shelters had a remarkable escape; while four other people sitting close to them were killed instantly, they were blown right through the other end of the shelter and escaped with only scratches. Rescue squads arrived at one devastated block of houses to find a small, grime-covered dog trying to scratch its way frantically into the middle of a jumble of debris, apparently seeking its master. Right through the night and until late the following day the dog mounted guard — but the dog's mistress, a little girl, was eventually accounted for and reunited with her pet.

Householders returned to their homes on Monday to salvage what they could, many taking away the remains of their possessions piled high on prams.

106-107. Marsh Road, Middlesbrough October 1940.

108. Back Argyle Street, Middlesbrough, October 1940.

The Enemy Was Not To Blame

Ironically, two of Middlesbrough's most spectacular wartime blazes were not the result of enemy action. The first happened on the night of Friday, 27 March 1942, when Binns' department store, at the corner of Newport Road and Linthorpe Road, became a mass of flames.

Exactly what caused it was never discovered, but it proved to be one of the town's most dramatic outbreaks of the war years, raging for over six hours, At its height, forty jets were being directed on the building and a complete curtain of water was thrown around it to protect neighbouring properties.

Millions of gallons of water were poured on to the flames, supplies from the mains being supplemented from the nearby Gilkes Street swimming baths and even from the river. Watched from a distance by large crowds, some 350 men of the NFS, with forty-eight fire appliances, tackled the blaze, but floor after floor of the building became enveloped and the roof collapsed.

Efforts turned to saving other property close by. Soldiers helped to rescue furniture and other goods from threatened premises. The Grand Electric Cinema, which then stood on the next corner, had been hurriedly cleared of patrons.

By morning, all that was left of the once elegant store was a smouldering, blackened, distorted shell on the island site between Linthorpe Road, Newport Road and Newport Crescent. Months later a British Restaurant was erected on the cleared area and it was not until eleven years after the war ended that Binns' present store, built on the same site, was opened.

Three months later, in mid-June, came another series of fires in the town centre — again not caused by enemy action.

This time, a thirteen-year-old fire-raiser was the culprit. He was committed to an approved school on a number of charges arising out of the firing of Upton's Store in Linthorpe Road, on Wednesday 17 June, and Dickson & Benson's (drapers and furnishers) and other premises twenty-four hours later.

Damage was estimated to total no less than one million pounds, making it Middlesbrough's most serious fire-loss on record, certainly up to that time.

Dickson & Benson had been established in the town for sixty years and occupied a large store which ran through from Linthorpe Road, where the C&A store now stands. Not only Dickson & Benson's store but about ten other shops around it were destroyed or badly damaged. They included Wilson's (known as *Cheap Wilson's*) milliners, Saltmer's (a high-class ladies' wear shop), Mason's (jewellers), Anthony Donald (men's wear), Burton's, Maypole Dairy, Charles (costumiers), W H Smith and Mansfield's. Binns, who had moved into temporary accommodation adjoining Dickson & Benson, suffered once again in the the Thursday outbreak. D&B's premises had an arcade running through from Linthorpe Road to Dundas Street and this acted as a wind tunnel, helping the blaze to spread rapidly. Fifty fire engines and almost five hundred firemen from many parts of North Yorkshire and South Durham fought the conflagration.

The rash of fires had caused grave concern in the town and when, after a further, small fire at the rear of a Linthorpe Road shop on the Friday (19th), a thirteen-year-old 'firewood pedlar' was apprehended, the relief was so great that the arrest was announced that evening in local places of entertainment.

Justice was swift. The following Tuesday the boy — described by the *Gazette* as 'an undersized, close-cropped youth in an open shirt, shorts and sandshoes" — appeared before the Juvenile Court, having admitted the offences, although he formally pleaded 'not guilty."

The Chief Constable, Alfred Edwards, prosecuted. He said the boy, who purchased wood which he re-sold as firewood, usually pushing it in an old pram, had admitted putting a match through an open door into a crate containing straw at the back of Dickson & Benson's. The shop was gutted. Temporary premises were occupied and the remainder of the Dundas Street property adapted as far as possible, but rebuilding was impossible because of the war.

109. Photograph from the *Evening Gazette* of 28 March 1942 taken at the height of the fire at Binns' Store.

110 The skeletal remains of Binns' Store, Middlesbrough. The fire was fought by no fewer than 350 NFS personnel with forty-eight appliances.

111. Aftermath of the fire which destroyed Dickson & Benson's Store in June 1942. The three-storey building in ruins in the centre of the picture is *Cheap Wilson's*. Dickson & Benson's, of which very little was left standing, lay behind it.
Picture courtesy of *Clinkard's*.

112. Damping down. The date and location of this picture is unknown but it is thought to be at either the Binns' or Dickson & Benson fires.

Back To The Air Raids.......

Middlesbrough's worst night for fatalities was 15-16 April 1942, when part of Newport was devastated by four bombs and twenty-eight people were killed. Another thirty-nine were seriously injured, according to official records. The dead included eleven children under the age of sixteen.

Carlow, Mills and Law Streets and Newport Recreation Ground, close by, bore the brunt of the attack. A twenty-four inch gas main was severed and caught fire, thirty-nine houses were wrecked and another 1,707 damaged — and 1,156 people were made homeless.

"One working man stood, a picture of grief, while one member after another of his family was brought out of the wreckage," reported the *Evening Gazette* grimly — although the paper was unable at that stage to name either the streets or even the town involved, because of censorship restrictions. The arrival of the first raider was so sudden that only a small number of people had been able to get into the shelters. Those who did were safe. Some shelters were scarred and cracked but even close to wrecked houses, none collapsed. People in bed were buried in debris while others were just preparing to go to the shelters. Several people were rescued, including an old man who was trapped under debris for over an hour. When rescue workers dragged him out he smiled and remarked: "Look after the others. I'm all right." He was more concerned about the loss of his pipe than his injuries. From all sides nothing but praise was accorded the Civil Defence services. People deprived of homes were accommodated in emergency sleeping and feeding centres and all night a mobile canteen played a useful part. Shop windows over a wide area were blown out.

Ironically, the same night more than twenty bombs were dropped in various parts of East Cleveland but there was only one fatality and other casualties were light. At Saltburn a stick of bombs fell across the town, giving it its worst raid of the war. Other bombs fell in the Marske and New Marske area, slightly damaging houses and farm buildings but causing no casualties. Old Skelton Mill was shattered when a bomb dropped in the orchard at the rear. Pigs in an outhouse near the mill were killed.

Thousands of incendiaries rained down over a wide area of Middlesbrough during a raid in the early hours of 7 July 1942, starting scores of fires, thirty-seven of which were attended by the NFS.

At Middlesbrough Girls' High School the caretaker, Mr H Richardson, and two form mistresses, Miss N R Barker and Miss M V Pearse, tackled the fire bombs with the aid of a stirrup pump until the arrival of the NFS, which found the building well alight. In spite of the damage there was no serious interruption in the pupils' schooling; the girls were transferred to another school.

Three churches were damaged in the attack—All Saints, St Aidan's and St George's Congregational. The Vicar of All Saints, the Reverend S Barker, saved his church and also the vicarage from destruction. He was on the roof of his house dealing with a firebomb when the roof of the church flared up. He gave the alarm and helpers rushed to assist in saving the church. Other properties were damaged in Linthorpe Road, Pelham Street, Portman Street, Percy Street, Victoria Road, Temple Street, Eldon Street, King Edward's Road, Clarendon Road, Amber Street, Garnett Street and Ruby Street. By prompt action, eight young people—six girls and two youths, all under eighteen—helped to save the Victoria Hall and other parts of the Co-operative Society's premises in Linthorpe Road. They tackled incendiaries which had plummeted through the roof and threatened the lower floors. During the raid bombs dropped in the Furness Shipyard at Haverton Hill; two hit and badly damaged the plater's shop, one fell alongside a ship, damaging it and the staging. Amazingly, considering the number of incidents and the widespread damage, there were few casualties. Three people were seriously injured, including a war reserve policeman who was struck by an incendiary, six were slightly injured and treated in hospital then sent home, and three more slightly injured people only required treatment at first-aid posts.

FIRE GUARDS get ready! FIREBOMB FRITZ is coming

Men and women of Britain's Fire Guard *will* be ready. Ready because during quiet times we train and practise, every day learning to do our job better. We're not asking for trouble, but we'll meet it properly when it does come.

FIRE GUARD TIPS.

No. 8 Don't enter a burning building or room unless you have something to attack the fire with.

No. 9 Keep all doors and windows shut at night as far as possible. Fire thrives on draughts or fresh air.

No. 10 If a burning room gets too hot for you, shut the door as you retreat. It cuts off the air supply. Besides, a door is a good fire stop.

BURN BRITAIN

BRITAIN SHALL NOT BURN!

ISSUED BY THE MINISTRY OF HOME SECURITY

116. Members of a Home Guard unit help the rescue services.

117-118. Damage to the Girls' High School, Middlesbrough. (now part of Teesside Polytechnic at the corner of King Edward's Road and Albert Road).

Middlesbrough town centre suffered its worst scenes of devastation in the early hours of Sunday, 26 July 1942. Beginning their attack at 1.33am, waves of German bombers swept over the area, scattering HE and oil bombs and incendiaries. Shops, stores, hotels, business premises and houses were destroyed or seriously damaged. Sixteen people died, some of them buried in the rubble of their homes, and more than eighty were injured. It was the town's highest total of casualties, although not the highest death roll for a single raid.

According to the official records, sixty-eight houses and seventy-six business premises were left "uninhabitable" and there was minor damage to 1,000 houses and 220 business properties. Two large stores (the Co-op and Eatons in Newport Road) were burned out. Gas and water mains were fractured and telephone communications interrupted.

The Wilson Street area bore the brunt of the attack. The Leeds Hotel, at the corner of Linthorpe Road and Wilson Street, was flattened and the landlord, his wife, son and maid, who had taken shelter in the basement, were all killed. It was four days before all the bodies were recovered.

Another bomb fell near the junction of Wilson Street and Albert Road and eight or nine shops were condemned as beyond repair. Five firewatchers whose base was wiped out had just left to go to offices for which they were responsible.

Councillor Fred Pette, general manager of the Co-operative Society and a divisional air raid warden, was on his way to Civil Defence headquarters when a bomb fell not far from his car, lifting it off the road and almost forcing him into a hedge. Recovering control and learning that shops were ablaze in Linthorpe Road, he drove there to find the food hall of the Co-op well alight. He dashed inside and from a window threw out all the books, documents and money that he could grab. Willing helpers carried them to safety.

With the aid of employees and others, Councillor Pette fought the flames until the NFS arrived. However, despite the attendance of forty fire pumps, the blaze spread from department to department, and floor to floor, until the Victoria Hall was completely enveloped. Part of the Clifton Street wall fell on to the new Emporium (later Disco), on the opposite corner, and that became involved, too. Damage was caused to the stock and the building, but two hundred people who had taken refuge in the strengthened basement of the Emporium were marshalled out to other shelters.

Twenty fire engines tackled a spectacular blaze at Theo Phillips' oil works in North Road. Years later Mr Bob Forrest, recalled that two-thirds of the firm's tank farm went up in flames.

"There were a dozen tanks at the Lloyd Street end of the works containing fuel oil and lubricating oils," he said. "They went up together with a building containing machinery where we made up hessian bags of grease for use in works. Fortunately, there was nobody in the works at the time so no lives were lost. When I was called out early the next morning the tanks were still smouldering — but we soon found other storage tanks and got back into full production, supplying the steelworks and collieries who were our main customers."

Incendiaries dropped on the North Riding Infirmary and when, a month later, official censors allowed the *Evening Gazette* to reveal details of the raid, it had a story to tell of "the heroism and fortitude" of a Dr P Baxter, a house surgeon there. The paper recounted that Dr Baxter left his bedroom clad only in pyjamas and dressing gown and found that three incendiaries had dropped on the roof of the maids' corridor. He scaled the drainpipe to reach the roof and when he realised the danger which threatened the building, he dashed over to another part of the roof, pulled the girdle off his dressing gown and, with the aid of helpers, hauled buckets of water to the roof and got the outbreak under control. By climbing through a trap door, other fire watchers

went to the doctor's aid. That job of work successfully accomplished, Dr Baxter dropped from one roof to another in order to save time and he badly sprained an ankle, but he was more concerned about other people's injuries than his own. Raid casualties began to arrive in increasing numbers and Dr Baxter helped other members of staff to treat them. Suddenly an urgent message arrived from the control centre asking for medical aid for a woman who had been trapped under the debris of a house in the Waterloo Road area. Dr Baxter was given permission to go. Because of the pain he was suffering, Dr Baxter was taken on a stretcher carrier and when he arrived on the scene of the demolished house he crawled down a hole to find the head and shoulders of an elderly woman protruding from the debris. He gave her an injection of morphia and later she was tenderly extricated from her plight and removed to hospital.

Though weary from his exertions, Dr Baxter started to hobble back to the infirmary but when he had got part of the way a police officer came to his aid by loaning him a bicycle. There was still more work for Dr Baxter to do at the infirmary. He helped to give medical aid to more raid victims. Monday revealed scenes of devastation throughout the central area of the town. Soldiers joined council workers and the emergency services in clearing the streets and sites, while members of the Home Guard helped the police and military to control traffic and sightseers. It was the first time the Home Guard had been called upon for this duty in the town. Seven months after the raid it was announced that an LNER shunter, Arthur Bradshaw, had been awarded the BEM and five of his colleagues had been commended "for brave conduct in Civil Defence" during an incident at the goods yard. "During the raid," said the citation, "bombs were dropped on and around the goods yard and fires were started. Bradshaw extinguished a number of incendiary bombs which had fallen into wagons and although bombs were falling and there was heavy anti-aircraft fire, he worked with an engine removing burning wagons."

All Will Be Trained to Fire Guard

COMPULSORY training for fire guards was announced by Miss Ellen Wilkinson, Parliamentary Secretary to the Ministry of Home Security, in a speech at Newcastle yesterday.

The scheme will apply to fire guards serving under the local authority and also to those at business and Government premises.

But the training will not be an extra liability, Miss Wilkinson pointed out. It will take place during the 48 hours of part-time service a month.

The recent "Baedeker" raids, said Miss Wilkinson, had shown very clearly how vital a part fire guards could play when an incendiary attack was made on a town.

"The National Fire Service," she went on, "naturally concentrate on the big fires that break out, and it then depends on the fire guards alone whether other serious fires start or whether this is prevented."

120. The Leeds Hotel on the morning of 26 July 1942.

122. Leeds Hotel, July 1942.

123-124 From the collection of John Proud. *above:* Wilson Street (looking towards Linthorpe Road), Middlesbrough, after the raid of 25-26 July 1942. *below:* Looking east. The Royal Exchange building is in the distance.

Lunchtime on a sunny August Bank Holiday Monday, 3 August 1942...

A crowded train had just pulled out of Middlesbrough railway station bound for the coast. A seventeen-year-old girl assistant at the station bookstall had closed for the afternoon and was taking unsold papers under the station subway back to the warehouse.

Above her, Tommy Marsden had driven the 11.20am express from Newcastle into the station, emptied his passengers and steamed off to a siding to uncouple his coaches. Now he was watching as another engine hauled them back into the platform for the 1.20pm return journey.

Meanwhile, elsewhere in the town, a young Dutch merchant seaman and his WAAF bride were preparing for their wedding at Middlesbrough Cathedral, just round the corner from the station. And in Wilson Street, 1,100 people, mostly women and children, were packed into the Hippodrome to see the matinee performance of the film *How Green Was My Valley*.

But at thirteen minutes past one, this peaceful holiday scene was abruptly shattered. Following quickly on the wail of the air raid sirens, a German Dornier 217 suddenly dived out of a low, dazzlingly white cloud and aimed four high explosive bombs at the station.

Two of them found their target, leaving a trail of devastation, with collapsed roof girders, a wrecked train and debris strewn throughout the station. One bomb fell immediately in front of the engine of the quarter full train, another on the buildings lining the down platform, used as a refreshment room, waiting room and facilities for guards and station staff.

A front buffer of the locomotive fell on a house 250 yards away. Wagons were derailed and heavy steel plates loaded on to them were flung against a stone wall.

A seventeen-year-old refreshment room boy died — the sixth member of his family to be killed in air raids on the town during the year. The guard on Tommy Marsden's train, who had decided to walk along the platform and cross the tracks in front of the engine, was also killed; years later, his son recalled that it should have been his father's day off, but he changed shifts to let a colleague off. An hour later and he would have finished his shift.

Tommy looked on in horror from the sidings then dashed to help. The train's new driver, from Gateshead, was standing on the platform and had survived, but his fireman was in the cab and was killed.

Tommy told the *Evening Gazette* many years later: 'There were folk still in the carriages. I got one fellow out and cleaned him up. Everything was chaos, a really rough do.'

The bookstall assistant, later to become Mrs Joyce Taylor, recalled: 'I was under the subway when the bombs came over. A young chap pushed my face against the wall. When we came back up, everything was bombed.'

Mrs Pamela Webb recalled, years later, how, as an eighteen-year-old, she was on duty in the booking office on the Redcar platform, covering between shifts. I heard the bomb whistling,' she told me. 'I was pretty lucky because the booking office was built into an arch. The bomb dropped on the refreshment room further along the platform. I went to go out of the door but some workmen dashed in and stopped me.

"If they had not done so, I would have gone down the steps to the subway — just as the tiled wall fell across the steps. The men took me across the tracks and through the damaged Newcastle train standing at the other platform. I was covered in dust and had tiny pieces of glass in my hair, but apart from being very shaken, I was all right."

At the Hippodrome, the air raid warning was broadcast from the front of the cinema — and largely ignored. Then came the explosions. "I went down into the audience," recalled the manager, Mr Norman Cox, looking back on the incident when he retired, "and told them it was an unexploded bomb from the week before. That's what I thought. I never realised the silly beggar had flown under the barrage balloons and bombed Middlesbrough railway station."

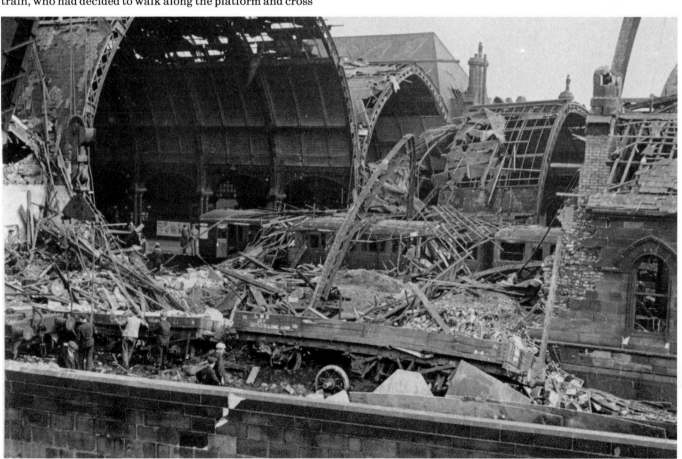

One bomb had, in fact, dropped in Crown Street, about fifty yards from the cinema entrance. The fourth had fallen on a fruit warehouse in Station Street. The total casualty list was seven dead, twenty-one injured and detained in hospital and thirty-five others less seriously injured.

Repair work was quickly put in hand and goods traffic was diverted to other routes. Telling the story under the headline "Remarkable clearance feat after Middlesbrough raid," the *Gazette* recorded — exactly three weeks later when censorship allowed — that freight traffic was moving through Middlesbrough again in under twenty-five hours and all passenger lines were back in operation within thirty-three hours.

The photograph at the bottom of the preceeding page is undoubtedly the most famous to come out of Teesside during the war, and was taken — as were many of the others in this book — by the then chief photographer of the *Evening Gazette*, Teddy Baxter.

He had just gone into the canteen on the top floor of the paper's Borough Road offices when the sirens sounded. Dashing out on to the roof, he was just in time to see the plane and the falling bombs.

"I rushed downstairs, jumped into a car and drove off towards the station," he recalled in 1980, just three years before his death. "On the way I had to drive through broken glass all the way down Albert Road from the Town Hall to the station; all the windows along that stretch had been blown out. I got three punctures — and the circulation manager, who was in charge of transport, played hell when I got back because tyres were hard to come by.

"In all, I 'dropped' ten plates, then rushed back to the office to develop and print them and get them on to a train from Darlington to London so that the censor could vet them. It was five-and-a-half weeks later before they were released for publication."

Subsequently, Ted's dramatic picture of the wrecked train and shattered station, with the first of the dead being carried off on a stretcher, went round the world. Enlargements, 20ft by 15ft, were sent to Australia and New Zealand to boost an appeal for clothing, blankets and other supplies for bombed-out families.

The photograph also appeared in an official booklet recording the story of Britain at war.

126. From the collection of John Proud.
above: The station looking south from Bridge Street. Preparations are under way to lift the damaged LMS wagons.

127. *below:* Looking east along the north side platform.

128. Another Teddy Baxter picture taken as repair work progressed.

Redcar

A bridge party was about to start its third rubber in a downstairs front room of Redcar's prestigious Zetland Club. A game of snooker had just ended upstairs and players were joining colleagues at the bar.

In all there were about eighteen people in the club around 9.30 that night — 21 October 1941— when tragedy struck in the shape of a direct hit from a high explosive bomb. Only six were to survive the devastation which followed.

Some of Redcar's leading citizens were among the twelve who died, trapped among the rubble. They included the Mayor, Alderman C Harris; Dr A S Robinson, whose house nearby was also destroyed; Mr Arthur Pickering, chairman of the local magistrates and a former managing director of the *Evening Gazette*; Mr Charles Herbert Goodwin, an optician with shops in Redcar and Middlesbrough; Councillor Joseph Roebuck, owner of a large drapery store in the town; Mr Frank Bainbridge, a builder; Mr John Barnett, a schoolmaster; bank manager Mr William Leslie Crozier; retired schoolmaster Mr Matthew Ranson; and Mr John Smallwood, commercial manager of an industrial firm.

The club stewardess, Mrs Mabel Fletcher, and a maid, Miss Doris Rigby, also died in the wreckage. The bridge players had amazing escapes. Troops helped emergency services with the rescue work. The *Evening Gazette* said the incident "will go down as the most tragic in the history of Redcar..."

It was believed at the time that the attacker had been surprised by a barrage from anti-aircraft guns recently placed on Yearby Bank after German bombers had several times tried to reach the works by "coming in the back way" over Guisborough. The plane on this occasion, it was suggested, probably jettisoned its bombs over Redcar before heading out to sea again. The same night a total of twenty-eight bombs fell over a wide area of East Cleveland. Considerable minor damage was caused at Brotton and North Skelton and to cottages and farm buildings near Lingdale. Fortunately, most of the bombs fell on open land — including four at Gribdale Gate, Great Ayton, and four more near Nunthorpe Church.

The main Whitby road was blocked at Loftus. One unexploded bomb fell on Gray's shipyard and another into the Tees near Malleable Wharf, Stockton.

The Zetland Club disaster was one of three major incidents at Redcar involving extensive loss of life. The other two followed daytime 'hit-and-run' raids on Dorman Long and Company's Warrenby Works.

These raids, on 15 November 1941, and 13 January 1942, caused the deaths of twenty workmen and serious injuries to more than seventy. On the first occasion two bombs dropped at about 9.30am while the sirens were sounding the alarm — the planes were apparently dive-bombing the works.

A new furnace which had taken two years to build and which had been started up four days previously was put out of action, suffering £9,600 worth of damage. A huge jib crane was bent almost in two. Three canaries used for gas detection survived in a small building opposite. Ten people were killed and forty-nine injured in this raid.

Four bombs fell during the January attack, damaging a steelworks plant, killing ten more workers and injuring thirty. The financial cost was later reported to company chiefs as £8,300.

About one hundred incendiaries rained down on the Redcar Lane - Borough Road area of Redcar early in the evening of 16 October 1942, but the many small fires which resulted were quickly dealt with and damage was slight. There were no casualties.

In the same raid bombs were dropped in fields in the Lackenby, Saltburn, Marske and New Marske areas. A rest centre was opened in the Church of England School at Marske to accommodate about twenty people whose houses had been damaged. The casualty list included three cows, two of which had to be slaughtered and the other 'treated' according to official records.

The last time bombs fell on the area was late on 22 March, 1943; they included 'firepots' (dual purpose bombs). Three houses were severely damaged and several suffered minor damage — and a water main fractured in the Zetland Road area. No-one was hurt, however.

About 240 incendiaries fell on the sands north of Redcar Wharf and more firepots on Warrenby Marshes. There were further bombs across an area stretching from Moorsholm to Upleatham. Two straw stacks were burned at Upleatham and part of the wing of a German plane was also found there.

A pigsty was hit when two HE bombs fell at Dormanstown on 2 September 1941 — but the occupants were out at the time! An oil bomb dislodged a tombstone in Coatham Parish Churchyard on 6 September 1940. And a year later two parachute mines fell on the rocks, shattering many windows.

Saltburn

Despite many hectic nights, the Saltburn, Marske and New Marske area suffered only two fatalities and twenty people injured as a result of air raids.

Saltburn's worst night was on 16 April 1942, when a stick of bombs fell across the town demolishing a surface air raid shelter and a row of shops were destroyed in Station Square. Fortunately, the shelter was unoccupied, but fifteen people in another just a few yards away suffered minor shock. Several houses in Exeter Street were badly damaged and it was here that the only civilian died.

The same night the old Skelton Mill was shattered when a bomb was dropped in the orchard at the rear. Pigs in an outhouse were killed, and four HE bombs fell near New Marske, damaging houses in the village and bringing down telephone wires, but causing no casualties. According to an *Evening Gazette* report, the roof of a double-decker bus on the Saltburn-to-Marske Road was blown off as the last of the bombs dropped in a field, but it continued its journey, its only two passengers little the worse for their experience. After a raid on 6-7 May 1941, the official record stated: "Bandstand reported destroyed in Italian Gardens (Saltburn) by HE bomb." Other, unofficial, notes mention the 'council school', Randolph Street area and a bungalow in Marske Road as having been hit.

Marske was ringed by incendiaries on one occasion. On 21 June 1940, the fire bombs struck wooden bungalows at Hummershill. During one raid the Vicar of Marske, the Reverend A H Waton, was in the village when he saw columns of smoke envelope his vicarage. A bomb had dropped ten yards from the front door.

131. Damage to a surface shelter in Middlesbrough.

Stockton

Stockton escaped relatively lightly from four years of air attack, but even so twenty-one people were killed, nine seriously injured and fifty-eight slightly hurt. Nearly two thousand houses were damaged, forty-one of them being totally destroyed. The town suffered 481 alerts and 67 HE bombs were dropped on it, two of them known to have been parachute mines. Many of the 1,400 incendiaries dropped fell on open countryside and did little damage.

The town's worst raids hit the Norton area during August, 1941. Bombs fell on Blue Hall Estate just at black-out time on a wet night on 15 August. The bodies from one house which received a direct hit were never recovered.

Three nights later, in the early hours of 19 August, a bomb dropped between two rows of houses in Pine Street and Benson Street, Norton. This time three people were killed and twenty-one injured. The first raid on the district, on Wednesday, 20 June 1940, saw a stick of bombs fall across Billingham Bottoms and one of Norton's oldest buildings, Norton Mill, mentioned in records of the district six hundred years ago, was damaged. It was being worked as a farm until the attack made it uninhabitable. Bombs which fell on the Northcote Street-St Peter's Road area of Stockton on 12 May 1941, damaged a water main, and an emergency order was issued warning people to boil all water before use. When the bell of Norton Parish Church rang the invasion call-out in one of the raids in the summer of 1940, all emergency services rushed to their posts — but the signal proved, fortunately, to be a false alarm.

In one of the last raids on the area, on 11 March 1943, three young German airmen who baled out from their plane after it had been crippled by a night fighter were captured in the Great Stainton district within two hours — with the Home Guard, the police and the National Fire Service each responsible for a capture!

We could lose the war by Fire! Be ready for FIREBOMB FRITZ

133. Bomb damage, Stockton.

Thornaby

The last serious raid on the Teesside area occurred before midnight on 11 March 1943, when South Bank, Thornaby and Stockton came in for punishment.

For Thornaby it was the most severe raid of the war, with three people killed and seventy-five injured, four of them seriously. Two parachute mines caused extensive damage to houses in Thornaby Road, George Street and Princess Street. An electricity sub-station received a direct hit, cutting off power to works in the vicinity which affected four thousand workers, and interrupted production for twenty-four hours, according to official records. There was extensive damage to Bon Lea Foundry and production was suspended "for some days." Water and gas mains burst, the latter catching fire. The Britannia Hotel and several adjoining houses were demolished. At the hotel, the six members of the Devine family, including three young children, escaped unhurt, although Mr Devine was buried in debris. Of the three fatal casualties, one was a woman warden, another a watchman, and the third was a man who was buried in the wreckage of his home.

Hundreds of homes were damaged, 86 beyond repair, and 350 people were made homeless. In the same raid, a man was killed at Stockton when a bomb fell immediately behind a watchman's hut at the end of Lawrence Street, just off Yarm Lane. The watchman himself escaped with shock but a lodger from Lawrence Street was killed when he went outside at the height of the raid to see what was happening. At South Bank, bombs fell in the town centre and caused considerable havoc. The police station and a sub-fire station in Normanby Road were hit and several small businesses badly damaged, while roofs and windows of houses over a wide area were shattered. The casualty role was two dead and twenty-one injured, eight of them seriously.

It proved a tragic night for a police superintendent and his family. One of the bombs crashed down in a street alongside South Bank police station, wrecking the part of the premises where they lived. The superintendent's wife and daughter were fatally injured and three other members of the family also suffered, chiefly from shock. In all, thirty-two houses were severely damaged in the town and five hundred sustained minor damage. During the raid an anti-aircraft shell exploded in Westbourne Road, Linthorpe, Middlesbrough, near to where two firewatchers were standing. Both died next day from their injuries and another man who was with them was seriously injured. Another AA shell wrecked a bungalow in Redcar Road, Marske, but no-one was hurt. Ironically, the three Linthorpe men were to prove to be Middlesbrough's last air raid casualties. A barge moored on the Tees opposite the Graving Dock was badly damaged and a watchman slightly hurt. At Saltburn a large crater was carved out by a bomb forty yards east of Toft signal cabin, close to the railway, but there were no casualties.

134. Wreckage from a house which was completely demolished by a bomb. Debris fell on this Anderson shelter — the shelter itself was left intact.

Skinningrove

Skinningrove Works was attacked by German bombers on numerous occasions and one daylight raider, after dropping a salvo of four bombs on the works, spent twenty minutes machine-gunning the streets of Loftus. Children making their way to school dodged from doorway to doorway as a Dornier roamed backwards and forwards overhead spraying bullets.

On another occasion a man died after being machine-gunned on his allotment.

In all about fifty casualties were recorded as a result of raids on the works.

The most destructive raid on the site occurred on 15 January 1942, when various parts of the plant were blasted and "serious loss of production" was officially logged.

Bombs and parachute mines fell within the Loftus Urban District on twenty-eight occasions, causing five deaths and 176 other casualties. On 15-16 April 1941, two parachute mines landed on the station footbridge causing extensive damage to windows and roofs in the vicinity of Church Row and Loftus Cottages — there were fourteen casualties.

Many bombs fell in open country, but in the autumn of 1940 there was a tragedy at Carlin How when a farmhouse was demolished. A man and wife lost their lives, but six other people escaped "miraculously"; a fifteen-year-old girl scrambled out of the wreckage and ran half-a-mile to fetch help.

Three bombs on Chapel Bank on 15 March 1941, damaged windows over a wide area and Loftus's Wesleyan Chapel was so badly hit it had to be pulled down.

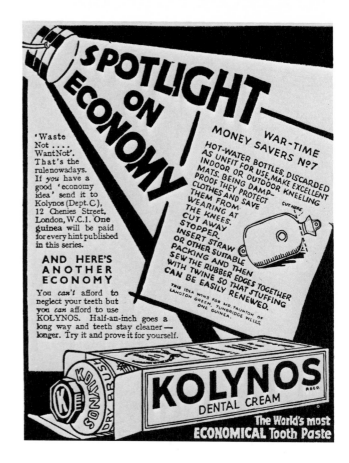

136. Skinningrove prewar.

Hartlepool

On the outbreak of war, special trains carried 8,000 schoolchildren, mothers and elderly from the Hartlepools to Scarborough, Stokesley, Whitby, Saltburn, Loftus, Guisborough and Filey, where it was felt they would be 'safe' from air attack.

Indeed, West Hartlepool became one of the first industrial towns in the North-east to suffer bombing. Four bombs fell on the Musgrave Street-Whitby Street area on 19-20 June 1940, but fortunately casualties were light. Although several shops and houses were demolished or damaged, only two people were killed and six seriously injured.

The Hartlepools had their worst ordeal in the summer of 1940, with the sirens sounding 147 times between July and September. In the early hours of 27 August, Church Street, West Hartlepool, was badly ravaged. Three people sheltering in a cellar were killed, shops were wrecked and the Clarence Hotel and Yorkshire Penny Bank severely damaged.

Two nights later, the Hartlepools bore the brunt of its most severe attack of that summer. Shortly before midnight, incendiary bombs fell over an area between Burn Road and Hutton Avenue. Then, at 4.35am, an enemy bomber heading for home released two bombs which fell on Pilgrim Street and Hilda Street. Of the forty-eight people killed in West Hartlepool, thirty-eight lost their lives in three raids — twenty-three of them on the night of 19 August 1941, when a heavy-calibre mine fell in Back Houghton Street and Elwick Road, also injuring seventy others and causing extensive devastation.

138. Church Street, West Hartlepool, 27 August 1940.
Picture courtesy of Cleveland County Council Libraries and Leisure Department.

Hitting Back

139. Members of a Northern Command anti-aircraft unit race to action stations.

140. Anti-aircraft Gun Operations Room, 30 AA Brigade, Elton Hall, Stockton-on-Tees.

141. A coast defence gun of 65 Medium Regiment opens fire from its hidden emplacement at Redcar.

Barrage balloons ringed Teesside to deter low-level attacks by German planes. One of them, affectionately nicknamed *Annie*, had a notable success on the evening of 15 January 1942, when it brought down a new type of Dornier bomber. The plane crashed on railway tracks at Clay Lane, South Bank, the crew dying in the inferno.

The incident earned a special mention in the HMSO publication, *Roof Over Britain*: "The balloon crew heard the aircraft approaching their site fast and low," it records. "Then they heard their balloon cable struck, but it was too dark to see the aircraft. The bomber crashed between one and two miles farther on and the balloon cable was recovered intact. A portion of the starboard wing of the enemy plane, cleanly cut by the impact, was subsequently recovered from a neighbouring site. The airman in charge of the site said, a day or two later: 'I've been putting balloons up and down, up and down, since October 1939, but it wasn't till this week that a real live Jerry went smack into my cable."

Watchers on the night of 19-20 June 1940, swore that a German raider picked his way through the balloon barrage to bomb the Acklam Wharf, Middlesbrough.

Four bombs were dropped, two on the wharf and two at the Ayresome Works of Rogers Mills & Co Ltd.

142-143. *above:* Aircraftsmen at a barrage balloon site prepare to ground a balloon to top it up with gas. *below:* Taken from the roof of the *Evening Gazette*. The exact date of the photograph is unknown but it was once thought to show the railway station under attack. However as the pall of smoke is coming from the wrong position for the railway station, it is now believed to show a barrage balloon on fire after being struck by lightning during a thunderstorm. It looks as if other balloons in the picture are being lowered. This is the only known photograph of Teesside's balloon barrage. The balloons were vulnerable during thunderstorms.

144. Flown from motorised winches, each balloon held around 19,000 cubic feet of highly flammable hydrogen gas. When inflated, a balloon measured approximately sixty-three feet by thirty-one feet and required a crew of two corporals and ten men, though this was later reduced to eight men. At the start of the war it took about forty minutes to raise a balloon to its operational height of around 6,000 feet.

145. Loading up trailers with gas cylinders for distribution to balloon sites. The Teesside balloon barrage was under the command of 33 Group RAF, with its headquarters at Newcastle-upon-Tyne, though this was later transferred to Hull, and then to Park Head House, Sheffield. In the middle of January 1941, the Air Officer Commanding, Balloon Command, was asked to consider the suggestion that the flying of balloons could be completely carried out by members of the Women's Auxiliary Air Force (WAAFs), despite the fact that the manning of balloons for twenty-four hours a day, frequently in the most appalling weather conditions, required physical strength not generally possessed by women. However, there had been a number of technical improvements to equipment, including the mechanisation of some aspects of handling balloons. Thus, one wet, cold morning in April 1941, twenty WAAF volunteers attended their first course at Cardington. By the end of June the women had proved their worth, and by the end of the year thousands of WAAF officers, NCOs and airwomen had been transferred to Balloon Command.

The first German plane to be brought down on English soil (*above*) crash landed near Whitby on 3 February 1940 — the first in Britain had been downed only hours earlier near Dalkeith, in Scotland.

The Heinkel III bomber had been attacking an unarmed fishing vessel off Whitby when three Hurricane fighters arrived on the scene. Crowds stood in the streets of Whitby watching the air battle develop. The planes crossed the coast and headed inland. One of the Hurricanes went in for the kill and the German pilot managed to force-land on the farm of Mr H Steele, near Sneaton Castle, a few miles from Whitby.

A policeman who was quickly on the spot, said later: "One of the crew tried to set fire to the plane with a Very light. It hadn't actually caught fire but was smoking. We used car fire extinguishers to put it out. We didn't know there were still two or three 500lb bombs in the place or we might not have been so keen!"

Years later the North Riding County Council erected a plaque (*right*) to commemorate the incident on a stone pillar at the junction of the moor road and the new road to Sleights.

The fighter pilot credited officially with the kill was Flying Officer (later to become Group Captain) Peter Townsend, whose name was to be linked romantically with that of Princess Margaret in the postwar years. Said a newspaper report, somewhat obviously: "The aeroplane might have made a much better landing had it not been for the fact that it struck a tree."

Over the next three years or so a number of German planes were brought down in the area around Teesside.

At 3.50pm on Sunday, 30 March 1941, a Junkers 88 of 1(F)/123 on a daylight reconnaissance mission ran into patrolling Spitfires of 41 Squadron over Middlesbrough and was shot down over Barnaby Moor, blowing up as it smashed into the ground. One German was found dead with his parachute entangled in a tree at Seaton but the rest of the crew were killed outright. lds, factories, A

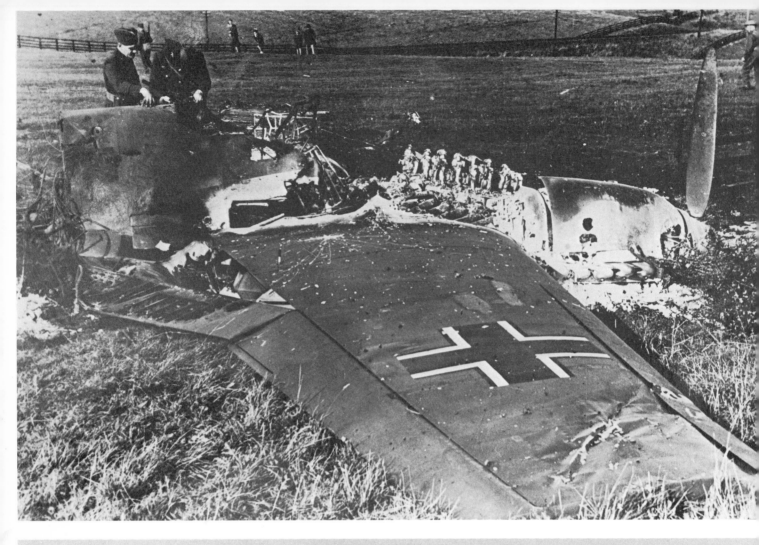

RAF Thornaby
by David Thompson

Thornaby acquired the status of an RAF Station Headquarters on 1 June 1937, in No 16 Group, Coastal Command.

Prior to this date, however, Thornaby had been in use since 17 March 1930, when No 608 (North Riding) Squadron, Auxiliary Air Force, formed there as a bomber squadron equipped with Avro-Lynx, followed by Westland Wapiti aircraft. In 1934, the squadron was transferred to No 12 Group, Fighter Command, and re-equipped with Hawker Demon aircraft, remaining at Thornaby as a lodger unit when control was passed to Coastal Command in 1937, et seq.

One month after becoming a Station Headquarters in July 1937, Thornaby became the base for numbers 224 and 233 Squadrons equipped with Anson aircraft. On 1 September 1938, Thornaby was transferred to No 5 Group, Bomber Command, and numbers 106 and 185 Squadrons equipped with Battle aircraft were based there; Coastal Command's Nos 224 and 233 Squadrons moved to Leuchars.

During the following two months the Station changed hands as follows - Bomber to Coastal and Coastal to Bomber, but on the outbreak of war in September, 1939, Thornaby was once again under Coastal Command control (No 18 Group) and remained so throughout the war.

Number 220 Squadron, equipped with Anson aircraft moved to Thornaby in August 1939, and commenced conversion on to Lockhead Hudson Mk1 aircraft. This was completed by December 1939. The squadron's main tasks were convoy escorts, reconnaissance patrols, and shipping strikes over the North Sea. The squadron's first action in World War Two took place on 13 September 1939, when one of its Anson's sighted and attacked a surfaced U-boat. Two attacks with single 100lbs anti-submarine bombs were made, but although very near misses were achieved the U-boat submerged and apparently escaped. The locating of the German prison ship *Altmark* is probably the best-known incident with which the squadron is associated in World War Two. The hunt for the *Altmark*, auxiliary and prison ship of the German pocket battleship *Graf Spee,* began early on 16 February 1940, after agents had indicated her presence off Norway. After an early morning briefing, three squadron Hudsons, K, M and V, took off from Thornaby to carry out a search for the Altmark off the Norwegian coast. Visibility ws bad at the start of the trip but it soon improved and the search area was in the order of forty miles. After searching for about two hours, Hudson K/220 located the *Altmark* at 1255 hours, and reported its position and continued to shadow the vessel until 1400 hours, when ships of the Royal Navy intercepted, boarded and released the Allied prisoners. The squadron's Hudsons had numerous combats with enemy aircraft during 1939-40 and altogether a total of eight enemy aircraft were claimed destroyed during this period. A rather

151. Avro Anson MKI of 233 Squadron based at Thornaby flew into Hunters Hill, Guisborough, in low cloud on 11 September 1937. Four crew were killed.

light-hearted note is injected into a report of an encounter between a squadron Hudson and an ME110 in which both aircraft were badly damaged; the crew of the Hudson were none the worse for the incident except the navigator, who remarked at the debriefing that he was now without a pencil — it had been shot out of his hand. The squadron also assisted in covering the evacuation from Dunkirk and flew anti-invasion patrols over the North Sea, eventually leaving Thornaby for Wick in April 1941.

Early in 1939, No 608 Squadron's role at Thornaby changed from Fighter to Coastal and the squadron re-equipped with Anson aircraft, becoming operational in the October in a convoy escort role. In the same month, the squadron received first deliveries of Blackburn Botha aircraft but these, proving operationally unsuccessful, were later withdrawn in favour of the former Ansons, to be followed first by Blenheims in the first half of 1941, and then Hudsons in the latter half. Three of the squadron's Hudsons attacked the port and airfield at Aalborg on 3 October 1941, and, throughout the rest of the month, other targets in Norway and Denmark. Leaflet dropping raids and strikes against enemy shipping off the Dutch coast were carried out with considerable success for the remainder of the year, when the squadron then moved to Wick.

Between 1941 and 1943, two Operational Training Units in succession were resident at Thornaby. No 6 OTU, commencing in July 1941, trained crews on Ansons and Hudsons. In June 1942, Hudsons of this OTU took part in a raid on Bremen from which one aircraft failed to return. Departing from Thornaby in March 1943, No 6 was replaced by No 1 OTU (Hudsons) until the latter Unit was disbanded in October 1943.

With the departure of N0 1 OTU, Thornaby came under the control of No 16 Group, Coastal Command. No 280 Squadron equipped with Warwick aircraft in the air/sea rescue role was also based there. Followed the next month (November) by No 281 equipped in the same role, however, this squadron was subsequently posted to Tiree in February 1944. No 280 Squadron moved base to Strubby at the end of April 1944, but left behind a detachment to operate from Thornaby. An incident worthy of note occurred on 23 March 1944, when a No 280 Squadron aircraft completed a successful operation at night by homing two British trawlers on to a dinghy in which were six members of a Halifax crew. A third air/sea rescue squadron, No 279, also equipped with Warwick aircraft, moved to Thornaby in November 1944, a small number of Hurricane aircraft being added to its establishment in early 1945; this squadron continued to operate from Thornaby until disbanded in March 1946.

No 608 (North Riding) Squadron (the first occupant of Thornaby) having previously been disbanded in August 1945, was re-formed at Thornaby in July 1946, in No 64 Group, Reserve Command. It was initially equipped with Mosquito aircraft but subsequently converted to Spitfires and later to Vampires. The squadron was eventually disbanded at Thornaby, together with all other Royal Auxiliary Air Force Squadrons, on 10 March 1957.

In October 1954, No 275 Squadron, in No 12 Group, Fighter Command, operating in the search and rescue role with Sycamore helicopters, was posted to Thornaby and operated there until being replaced by No 92 Squadron equipped with Hunters, in No 13 Group, Fighter Command in September 1957. No 92 Squadron departed from Thornaby in October 1958, and the Station was reduced to a care and maintenance basis, the airfield being closed completely.

A system of decoy airfields, factories, shipyards, coke ovens and railway marshalling yards was established throughout the country by the RAF to draw off enemy bombers. One decoy was set up in a field at Greatham, while a mock airfield sprang up on open land just off the trunk road east of Grangetown — on part of what is now ICI Wilton and where Foxcover Lane used to run. The "airfield" was complete with dummy wooden planes.

153. On 8 November 1939, a Coastal Command Lockheed Hudson of 220 Squadron, crashed into a house in Cambridge Road, Linthorpe, Middlesbrough. All four crew members were killed.

154. This was the scene after a Coastal Command Lockheed Hudson, heading back home to Thornaby aerodrome, crashed into a house in Cambridge Road, Linthorpe, Middlesbrough — just west of Thornfield Road junction — on 8 November 1939.

All four crew members were killed but the occupants of the house escaped; they were apparently at the rear of the house when the plane hurtled into the front. Eyewitness Norman Ferguson was cycling home from school along Thornfield Road with a friend at about four o'clock in the afternoon when the drama occurred. "There was nothing to indicate it was in difficulties," he remembers. "No trail of smoke or anything like that. There was a bang and masses of wreckage flew into the air. We cycled back and watched from near Grey House. The emergency services seemed to be on the scene almost at once."

One reason for the prompt response was that an AFS crew, already out on other duties, had seen the plane limping home, realised it was in trouble — and followed it. One of the senior fire officers on the spot was Bill Taylor. "The plane had gone through the roof of one of a pair of semi-detached houses," he recalled. "Petrol had run down underneath the floors and into the foundations. The whole house was in flames and as we were putting the fire out, the petrol below kept re-igniting with small explosions and blowing us out. The plane still had a bomb on board and we found it in the under-drawing of the house — sliced clean in two."

155. Two of the pilots who took part in the location of the *Altmark*. The picture was not released for publication until Tuesday 20 February 1940.

156. Thornaby Aerodrome 1940. The view is to the north-east with Thornaby Road in the foreground. Note the camouflaged runways. Thornaby was one of the first stations to have decoy airfields, one at Grangetown, the other at Middleton. Both were equipped with dummy buildings and aircraft. Both were abandoned early in the war. In the early hours of 6 June 1940, a cheeky — or enterprising — German raider slipped in with our own planes while they were carrying out a bombing exercise and bombed the aerodrome at Thornaby (situated where the new town centre now stands). Two Lockheed Hudson aircraft were set ablaze, together with a building — and an airman later died of his wounds.

157. Blackburn Botha aircraft. For the first two years of the war, 608 Squadron was equipped with Ansons, Bothas, and Blenheims, their operational role being convoy escort.

158.*Right* A flight of Bothas in formation. These aircraft were equipped with Bristol Perseus engines and carried torpedoes.

159. Avro Anson MKI on a coastal patrol sortie out of Thornaby, 1939.

61. Wing Commander Peter Derek Roughier Hutchings, 608 (North Riding) Squadron, was awarded the DSO. Although charged with the responsibilities of administering and operating his squadron, Wing Commander Hutchings also took part in operational sorties. At this time 608 Squadron were employed on anti-shipping strikes and offensive patrols over enemy coastal areas.

162. 608 (North Riding) Squadron Hudson crew hold a last minute conference before setting out on a mission.

164. Spitfire bought for the RAF by Middlesbrough.

165. Beaufighter flying on one engine. In May 1945, Beaufighters of 455 Squadron Royal Australian Air Force, operating from Thornaby, attacked German minesweepers in Kiel Bay. On 7 May, Coastal Command issued orders to cease attacks on enemy shipping.

166. A Vickers Warwick of 279 Squadron. In October 1943, Thornaby became the home of the Air Sea Rescue Training Unit where it received its Warwicks. The Warwick carried a lifeboat in its bomb bay. At Thornaby 279, 280 and 281 Squadrons were either re-equipped or re-formed as ASR Squadrons. After the war, the airfield continued to be used by the RAF and an ASR detachment remained until June 1946.

167. Warship Week, March 1942, raised a total of £886,471 and resulted in Middlesbrough adopting the Hunt class escort destroyer HMS *Cleveland*. Built by Yarrow, *Cleveland* was launched in April 1940, displaced 907 tons, and her 2-shaft geared turbines gave her a maximum speed of around 26 knots. In 1943 she was transferred to the Mediterranean with her sisters *Atherstone*, *Hambledon*, *Mendip*, *Quantock*, *Lynedale* and *Whaddon*. The photograph dates from 1945 and depicts *Cleveland* in Trieste harbour. *Cleveland's* end came in June 1957 when she was wrecked en route to a shipbreaker's yard.

168. Miss Joyce Hoyle of Camden Street, Middlesbrough, joins the ATS.

170. ATS military police being inspected by Junior Commandant Jill MacDermott 1942.

171. Horse lines of the Yorkshire Hussars outside Jerusalem. The Yorkshire Hussars formed part of the 5th Cavalry Brigade (1st Cavalry Division), with the Queen's Own Yorkshire Dragoons and the Sherwood Rangers Yeomanry. In October 1939, the brigade moved to Lincolnshire where it was brought up to full strength with additional reservists and officers from the Inns of Court Regiment. Two months later, the 1st Cavalry Division was posted to Palestine.

172. A Cruiser MKIII (A13) tank of the Yorkshire Hussars stopped dead in its tracks, by ox power. The MKIII entered service with regular cavalry units in 1939. It weighed fourteen tons, was powered by a 340hp Liberty/Nuffield aero-engine and was armed with a two-pounder gun and a co-axial machine gun. The design incorporated Christie suspension, the independently sprung wheels, giving the four-man crew a remarkably smooth ride even when the tank was travelling flat out at 30mph. .

173. An unarmed Valentine (Infantry Tank MKIII) of the Yorkshire Hussars leads a column through a Cypriot village. The Yorkshire Hussars were the first armoured regiment to be based on the island. Photograph by Lieutenant Tuaner.

THE GREEN HOWARDS

175. 1st Battalion The Green Howards detraining at Richmond station on their return from Palestine in 1939. In August 1939, the battalion was at Catterick, (as part of the 15th Brigade), under the command of Lieutenant-Colonel Robinson. On 4 October, they sailed with the BEF for France, but were withdrawn in April 1940 and sent to Norway, returning to England shortly afterwards.

176. Signals Platoon, 2nd Battalion, Ferozepore. The battalion served overseas throughout the war including Jubbelpore, Razmak, Peshawari, Lochardga, Arakan and Goppe Bazaar. In 1945 they were at Chittagong, Kyaukpyu, Minbyin, Gonchwein and Pyin Wan.

177. The photographs on this page are dated 28 January 1940 and were part of a propaganda series for home consumption. The troops are from either the 4th or 5th (Territorial) Battalions The Green Howards, which together with the 4th Battalion East Yorkshire Regiment formed the 150th Brigade, 50th (Northumbrian) Division.

178. Transport assemblies at the quayside. On arrival in France, the 4th Battalion went to Conlie, the 5th Battalion to Rouez. On 16th May 1940, both battalions began their retreat towards Dunkirk.

179. Marching away to a rest camp. Following Dunkirk, the 4th and 5th Battalions were re-equipped and brought up to strength. On 23 April 1941, they were embarked at Liverpool for the Middle East via South Africa. The end of November 1941 saw them in Egypt, crossing the Libyan frontier on 27 January 1942. In June 1942 a major German offensive against the Gazala Line saw the two battalions being slowly strangled by the encircling forces and they finally went under in the heat and dust of the notorious Cauldron. However, battalion cadres under Major Lacy reached Sidi Bengallad and 69 Brigade. In July the cadres were sent to the infantry brigade depot where they joined 'Z Brigade' in the Cairo defence scheme. In September cadres were reduced to two officers and ten other ranks and embarked for England arriving in November 1942. On arrival at Richmond the cadres were disbanded. The 4th and 5th Battalions The Green Howards ceased to exist.

right: Prisoners of war. Members of the 5th Battalion, The Green Howards, pictured in December, 1943 at Stalag 344 in Germany, prior to going out to work in the coal mines at Arnowitz. Contributed by Mr. Stan Ward, of Carlin How, East Cleveland, who was a POW from 1942 to the end of the war and is fourth from the left in the back row (with muffler, under letter 'S').

181.*below*: War Weapons Week, Redcar. The Green Howards provide the music.

182.*below*: Training at home in the late summer of 1940. Members of the 7th Battalion The Green Howards take up their positions in a pill-box during an anti-invasion exercise. The 7th Battalion was embodied at Bridlington in August 1939 under the command of Lieutenant-Colonel Richmond-Brown and along with the 6th Battalion and the 5th Battalion East Yorkshire Regiment, formed 69 Brigade of the 23rd Division commanded by Major-General Herbert. The 69th Brigade went to France in April 1940, retreating to Dunkirk on 16 May. On 31 May they embarked at Gourock for the Middle East via South Africa and Cyprus. This brigade also fought on the Gazala Line, and like the 4th and 5th Battalions, found themselves surrounded. However, in a daring night break-out to the west, the brigade succeeded in passing through the enemy's front line and rear areas to reach Hacheim.

183-184. North Africa. Members of the 1st Battalion Green Howards in a wadi. *below*: Bren carriers of the 1st Battalion, Anzio offensive. The battalion landed in Italy in September 1943, serving at Picerno, the Biferno and Sangro Rivers, Lanciano, Minturno and Trimonsvoli before embarking for the Anzio Beachhead where they arrived on 2 March. In the small hours of 23 May, the Green Howards led the diversionary attack out of the beachhead, a few hours before the main attack against Cisterna.

185. Members of B Company, 1st Battalion The Green Howards, Palestine, July 1944.

186-187. These photographs from the Inter Service Public Relations Directorate, India, show members of the 2nd Battalion, The Green Howards, on patrol in Burma, 1944.

188. The 6th Battalion collect their forty-eight hour ration packs and check their weapons.

189. Preparations for D Day. Exercise Fabius, May 1944.

192-193. The 6th and 7th Battalions embarked for France.
right: A 6pdr gun in action in the Lingevres area 16 June 1944.

194. The 12th Battalion, The Green Howards, can trace its history back to January 1940 when 5 Holding Battalion was formed at Wetherby under Lieutenant-Colonel Bright. In June 1940 the unit was re-designated 50 Green Howards and in September became the 12th Battalion, The Green Howards, and was stationed at Redcar. In August 1942 the unit converted into 161 Reconnaissance Regiment (Green Howards) and was based at Scarborough. After service in Northern Ireland, B Squadron went to Normandy under Major Graham.

195. CSM Hollis

196. CSM Hollis (with stick) Paris c1944

195-196. In Normandy on 6th June, 1944, during the assault on the beaches and the Mont Fleury battery, CSM Stanley Hollis's company commander noticed that two of the pill-boxes had been by-passed and went with CSM Hollis to see that they were clear. When they were twenty yards from the pill-box, a machine gun opened fire from the slit and CSM Hollis instantly rushed straight at the pill-box, recharged his magazine, threw a grenade in through the door and fired his Sten gun into it, killing two Germans and making the remainder prisoner. He then cleared several Germans from a neighbouring trench.

By his action he undoubtedly saved his company from being fired on heavily from the rear and enabled them to open the main beach exit.

Later the same day in the village of Crepon the company encountered a field gun and crew armed with Spandaus at 100 yards range. CSM Hollis was put in command of a party to cover an attack on the gun but the movement was held up. Seeing this, CSM Hollis pushed right forward to engage the gun with a PIAT from a house at fifty yards range. He was observed by a sniper who fired and grazed his right cheek and at the same moment the gun swung round and fired at point blank range into the house. To avoid the falling masonry CSM Hollis moved his party to an alternative position. Two of the enemy gun crew had by this time been killed and the gun was destroyed shortly afterwards. He later found that two of his men had stayed behind in the house and he immediately volunteered to get them out. In full view of the enemy who were continually firing at him, he went forward alone using a Bren gun to distract their attention from the other men. Under cover of his diversion, the two men were able to get back.

Wherever fighting was heaviest CSM Hollis appeared and in the course of a magnificent day's work he displayed the utmost gallantry and on two separate occasions his courage and initiative prevented the enemy from holding up the advance at critical stages.

It was largely through his heroism and resource that the company's objectives were gained and casualties were not heavier and by his own bravery he saved the lives of many of his men.

Daily Mirror
MAY 8
Tuesday, May 8, 1945
No. 12,911
Registered at G.P.O. as a Newspaper.
ONE PENNY

VE-DAY!

IT'S OVER IN THE WEST

TODAY is VE-Day — the day for which the British people have fought and endured five years, eight months and four days of war.

With unconditional surrender accepted by Germany's last remaining leaders, the war in Europe is over except for the actions of fanatical Nazis in isolated pockets, such as Prague.

The Prime Minister will make an official announcement—in accordance with arrangements between Britain, Russia and the U.S.—at 3 o'clock this afternoon. ALL TODAY AND TO-MORROW ARE PUBLIC HOLIDAYS IN BRITAIN, IN CELEBRATION OF OUR VICTORY.

We also remember and salute with gratitude and pride the men and women who suffered and died to make triumph possible — and the men still battling in the East against another cruel enemy who is still in the field.

War winners broadcast today

You will hear the voices of the King, Field-Marshals Montgomery and Alexander, and General Eisenhower when they broadcast over the B.B.C. Home Service to-night.

After the King's speech, at 9 p.m. and organised from it by the news bulletin, comes "Victory Report," a special programme which will contain the recorded voices of Mr and Monty and other famous personalities of the war.

Additional features of the B.B.C. Home programme, which will end at 1 a.m. to-morrow include, at 8 p.m. an address by the Archbishop of Canterbury at a Thanksgiving Service for Victory, and at 8.50 a tribute to the King.

VE-SCENE
TRAFALGAR SQUARE

It was a high old time in Trafalgar-square last night. Everybody wanted to climb something. This party of Wrens and Allied soldiers celebrated by clambering on to the lions. Army policemen present like Nelson on his column turned a blind eye.

London had joy night

"Daily Mirror" Reporter

Piccadilly Circus, VE-EVE.

THIS is IT and so are all going mad. Since on Oronteous of us in Piccadilly-circus. The police saw more than 10,000 and that's a conservative estimate.

We are dancing the Conga and the jig and "Knees up Mother Brown," and we are singing and whistling, and blowing paper trumpets.

The idea is to make a noise. We are Eros above the roar of the motors of low-flying bombers "shooting up" the celebrating Londoners.

We have been waiting from two o'clock to celebrate. We went home at six when the word that the news of VE-Day would never come, but we are back now.

And on a glorious night we are making the most of it. A paper hatted throng is trying to pull me out of this telephone box. A light, but from the door tight, but the din from Piccadilly Circus is drowning my voice.

It is past midnight. We are still singing. A group of men above the crowds as the American army swarmed in.

Continued on Back Page

197. *top right:* A victory bonfire.

199. *right:* Woodhay Avenue, Whinney Banks, Middlesbrough, won first prize in VE Week for the best dressed street. The picture belongs to Mrs Norma Pearson, who is in the middle with the long plait.

200. VE Day party in the front garden of a house in Eden Road Grove Hill, Middlesbrough. (Taken by Mr Harold Thompson)

201. VE Day service, Albert Park, Middlesbrough.

202. Workmen demolish shelters in Costa Street, South Bank.

How Teesside Fared

The table below gives the 'vital statistics' of air raids on Teesside and the surrounding area during World War Two. They are based principally on information issued by the Civil Defence officers in the various local authority districts towards the end of the war. Where there are blanks this is because it has not proved possible to track down the figures.

AREA	NO OF ALERTS	NO OF BOMBS DROPPED	OCCASIONS BOMBS DROPPED	CASUALTIES	DAMAGE
Middlesbrough County Borough	481	135 HE's — Incendiaries on 12 occasions	23	78 killed, 172 seriously injured, 422 slightly injured	318 buildings destroyed, 1,210 damaged, 7,337 houses slightly damaged
Billlingham Urban District				15 killed, 21 seriously injured, 49 slightly	
Eston Urban District (including South Bank and Grangetown)	480	107 HE's 489 incendiaries	22	33 killed, 24 seriously injured, 67 slightly injured	2,212 properties damaged of which 53 houses demolished
Guisborough Urban District	481	63 HE's 1,120 incendiaries	21	None	26 properties damaged (slight damage from blast)
Loftus Urban District	481	HE's dropped for first time 3.7.1940	28	5 killed, 16 seriously injured, 160 slightly	600 buildings
Redcar Borough	479	83 HE's, 2 parachute mines, numerous incendiaries	26 1st bombs 27.6.1940	34 killed, 36 seriously injured, 26 slightly (1st death Tod Point Rd, Warrenby 8 May 1941	1,538 buildings damaged and destroyed
Saltburn and Marske Urban District	480	114 HE's, 37 'fire pots'. Inceniaries' too numerous to mention'.		2 killed 26 injured	1,120 properties of which 30 houses destroyed or had to be demolished
Skelton and Brotton Urban District	480	98 HE's, 3 landmines, Incendiaries on 8 times		2 killed (at Crag Hall Farm, Brotton), 1 injured	67 houses and 14 other buildings demolished
Stockton Borough	481	67 HE's, 2 parachute mines, 1,400 incendiaries		21 killed, 9 seriously injured, 58 slightly	Nearly 2,000 houses damaged of which 41 totally destroyed
Thornaby Borough				5 killed, 7 seriously injured, 73 slightly	
Hartlepool Borough	481		7 when damage or casualties caused	22 killed 93 injured	22 houses destroyed, 72 seriously damaged 1,677 slightly damaged
West Hartlepool	481		36	48 killed, 16 seriously injured, 173 slightly	106 buildings destroyed, 5,639 damaged (mostly houses & shops, public buildings including churches Factories, Hotels)
North Riding of Yorkshire **	480		418	139 civilians killed 618 injured ***	Substantial damage at Thornaby, South Bank, Grangetown, Redcar, Whitby, Scarborough, Flaxton, Loftus, Saltburn and Masham. In all 15,317 buildings damaged.

* The total of 70 deaths in the Hartlepools during the whole of the war contrasted with the 127 who died in 50 minutes on 16 December 1914 during the famous bombardment by German warships)

** Includes Eston, South Bank, Grangetown, Redcar, Saltburn, Marske, Skelton, Brotton, Loftus, Thornaby and Whitby.

*** Fatal casualties occurred at Thornaby, South Bank, Grangetown, Redcar, Whitby, Scarborough, Skelton, Loftus, Saltburn, Flaxton, Masham and Thirsk. (Figures do not include casualties due to own aircraft accidentally crashing).

203. Older brother takes charge. Evacuees at Stokesly.

204. Reginald Hebden with an early ARP rescue lorry.

Fact File

1939

Mar 24   Britain and France guarantee Poland's frontiers.

Apr 3   Hitler orders Wehrmacht to prepare to invade Poland.

Aug 29   Hitler announces that he will negotiate on Poland providing an emissary arrives in Berlin by noon the following day. Hitler's demands are rejected.

Aug 31   At 4pm Hitler orders the invasion of Poland to commence at dawn the following day.

Sep 1   German forces invade Poland. Italy proclaims non-belligerent status. Scandinavian countries and the Baltic States declare their neutrality. Evacuation of children from British towns and cities begin.

Sep 3   Britain and France declare war on Germany. India, Australia and New Zealand declare war on Germany. Belgium declares her neutrality. Last day of evacuations in Britain. SS *Athenia* torpedoed and sunk by a U-boat in contravention of direct order from Hitler.
Nationwide air raid alerts.

Sep 4   Advance units of the BEF land in France.

Sep 5   Middlesbrough ARP sub-committee begins daily meetings.

Sep 8   4,963 unaccompanied schoolchildren, 650 mothers and children and 605 others evacuated from Middlesbrough.

Sep 10   Canada declares war on Germany.

Sep 17   Soviet Russia invades Poland.

Sep 27   Poland surrenders.

Sep 29   Russia and Germany formally divide Poland

Oct 6   Hitler offers a peace settlement to Britain and France.

Oct 11   BEF strength stands at 158,000 men.

Oct 12   Hitler's peace proposals rejected.

Nov 8   Assassination attempt on Adolf Hitler fails.
Hudson bomber of 220 Squadron crashes on to a house at Linthorpe.

Nov 30   Russia invades Finland.

Dec 3   Conscription in Britain is extended to all males aged 19-41. Females aged 20-30 are required to work as auxiliaries or on defence jobs.

Dec 29   Finns defeat the Russians at Suommusalmi.

1940

Jan 8   Rationing of basic food stuffs begins in Britain.
Finns defeat Russians at Karelin.

Feb 11   Russia launches a massive attack on Finland.

Feb 17   400,000 more children evacuated from British cities.

Mar 12   Russian-Finnish war ends.

Mar 29   Russia declares her neutrality in the European war.

May 10   Germany invades the Low Countries.

May 13   Germany invades France. Liege falls.

May 18   Antwerp falls to the Germans.

May 25	Teesside becomes the first industrial area in England to be attacked by German aircraft.
May 26	Evacuation of allied troops from Dunkirk begins.
June 10	Neville Chamberlain resigns and is replaced as Prime Minister by Winston Churchill.
June 14	Anthony Eden appeals for men to join the Local Defence Volunteers.
June 17	France sues for peace.
June 18	Italy declares war on France and Britain.
June 19/20	Middlesbrough attacked by lone raider, four bombs dropped.
June 20	Bombs dropped across Billingham Bottoms.
June 21	Incendiaries dropped on Marske.
June 27	Raid on Middlesbrough — Transporter, St Peter's Church, Town Hall etc.
July 2	Hitler issues orders for the invasion of Britain.
July 19	Hitler offers peace terms to Britain.
Aug 15	Luftwaffe launch an all-out assault in an attempt to cripple the RAF.
Aug 28	First Middlesbrough death from enemy action when bombs drop on Grove Hill area.
Sep 7	London Blitz begins.
Oct 3	Neville Chamberlain, now a very sick man, resigns from the Government.
Oct 13	Middlesbrough's heaviest raid to date. Twenty-one people killed, thirty seriously injured, seventy-two slightly hurt.
Oct 28	Italy invades Greece.
Nov 8	Greeks defeat the Italians.
Nov 9	Chamberlain dies.
Nov 14-15	Coventry devasted in an eleven hour raid.

1941

Jan 21	*Daily Worker* closed down under the Defence Regulations. Tobruk falls to British and Australian troops.
Feb 12	German troops land at Tripoli.
Feb 16	Bombs dropped on South Bank, twelve people killed.
Apr 5	German troops invade Greece.
Apr 15-16	Two parachute mines seriously damage part of ICI Billingham.
Apr 20	Greeks surrender.
May 7	Incendiary raid over a wide area from Saltburn to Middlesbrough.
May 10	Rudolf Hess lands in Scotland.
May 12	Glebe Road area of Middlesbrough hit by HE bomb.
May 16	Lone raider causes a spectacular fire when one of its bombs scores a direct hit on a gas holder on the north side of Middlesbrough. Firemen clapped clay over the holes as holder "burned like a huge gas ring."
June 15-16	Parachute mines dropped within Loftus Urban District.
June 19	Visit to Middlesbrough by the King and Queen.
June 22	Germany invades Russia on a 1,800 mile front. Clothes rationing introduced in Britain.

205. The 8th Middlesbrough Company Boys' Brigade spent their Easter Holiday of 1942 collecting salvage.

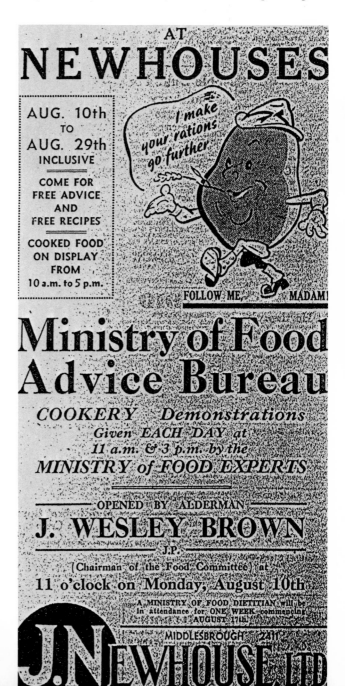

208. Practice makes perfect. Practice tests were carried out
for street fire-fighting parties at Grove Hill in April 1942.
This picture from the *Evening Gazette* shows a party tackling an incendiary device in Nut Lane.

Aug 15	Blue Hall Estate, Stockton, hit by HE bombs.
Aug 18	National Fire Service formed.
Sep 2	German troops within twenty miles of the Kremlin.
Sep 22	*'Tanks for Russia Week"* begins in British arms factories.
Oct 21	Redcar's worst night of the war. The prestigious Zetland Club takes a direct hit. Only six survivors. Several of Redcar's leading citizens killed including the mayor.
Nov 15	Redcar bombed.
Dec 1	German armour within nine miles of the Kremlin.
Dec 7	Japanese carrier planes attack the American Pacific Fleet at Pearl Harbour.
Dec 8	The United States and Britain declare war on the Empire of Japan.

1942

Jan 13	Redcar bombed.
Jan 15	Teesside balloon barrage succeeds in bringing down a raider, which crashed on to railway tracks at Clay Lane.
Feb 15	Singapore falls to the Japanese.
Apr 15-16	Newport devastated by HE bombs. 28 people killed in Middlesbrough's worst night for fatalities. Also Saltburn's worst attack.
June 21	Tobruk falls to Rommel.
July 7	Major incendiary raid on Middlesbrough, Billingham, Stockton and Hartlepool.
July 26	Middlesbrough town centre suffers its worse scenes of devastation in an attack beginning at 1.33 am.
Aug 3	August Bank Holiday Monday. Middlesbrough railway station badly damaged by HE bombs.
Aug 19	Canadian and British raiding forces land at Dieppe.
Aug 25	The Duke of Kent is killed in a plane crash.
Sep 6-7	Last German bombs to be dropped on Middlesbrough.
Oct 16	Incendiaries dropped on Redcar. Little damaged done.
Nov 4	Afrika Korps defeated by the 8th Army at El Alamein.

1943

Feb 2	German 6th Army surrenders at Stalingrad.
Mar 11	Last serious raid on Teesside area when South Bank, Thornaby and Stockton come in for punishment.
May 12	Surrender of Axis forces in North Africa.
May 16	Third Birthday parade Home Guard: 8th and 9th Battalions parade at Albert Park; 19th (Stockton) Battalion at Ropner Park.
July 10	Allies land in Sicily.
July 24	RAF attack Hamburg with 740 planes.
July 25	RAF attack Essen with 627 planes.
July 27	RAF attack Hamburg with 739 planes. 20,000 men, women and children are thought to have died.
Sep 8	Italian surrender made public, though a secret armistice had been signed on the 3rd.
Oct 13	Italy declares war on Germany.

1944

Jan 22   Allies land at Anzio.
June 6   Allies land in Normandy.
June 22 Russia launches her summer offensive on a 300 mile front.
July 24 'Hitler salutes' made mandatory form of salute in the German Army.
Aug 25   Liberation of Paris.
Sep 17   Lights go on again in Middlesbrough.
Sep 30   Part demobilisation of the National Fire Service begins. The released came under the Ministry of Labour and National Service and were liable to be called up for the armed forces or be directed to industry dependent on their age.
Nov 18   Last bomb to be dropped on Middlesbrough lands on allotments between Rockliffe Road and Acklam Road North. About 100 houses and a dairy damaged. It was dropped by accident from an Allied plane due to a 'hang up'.
Dec 13   Home Guard stood down.

1945

Feb 13   RAF attack the Brabag Oil Plant with 3 planes. However, this is only a diversionary raid for the main thrust is against the undefended city of Dresden. 773 planes are used in the attack and an estimated 135,000 civilians are killed.
Mar 7   United States troops cross the Rhine at Remagen.
Apr 1   Cheese ration cut.
Apr 12   Roosevelt dies.
Apr 23   Blackout restrictions lifted.
Apr 25   US and Soviet troops meet on the Elbe.
Apr 28   Mussolini and his mistress are executed by Italian partisans.
Apr 29   German forces in Italy surrender.
Apr 30   Adolf Hitler commits suicide.
May 1   Last ARP workers given a month's notice.
May 4   Surrender of German forces in North West Europe.
May 7   Unconditional surrender of all German forces.
May 22   Rations cut again.
May 23   Churchill resigns and forms a caretaker government.
June 12 Middlesbrough ARP sub-committee disbanded.
July 5   General Election.
July 22 Tea ration increased.
July 26 Labour Party sweeps to victory with 393 seats.
Aug 6   Atom bomb dropped on Hiroshima.
Aug 9   Atom bomb dropped on Nagasaki.
Aug 14   Japanese surrender.
Sep 1   Clothing ration cut by 25 per cent.
Sep 19   William Joyce (Lord Haw Haw) sentenced to death for treason.
Oct 23   Income Tax reduced from 10s to 9s in the pound.
Dec 20   Labour controls end.

209. Lady Dorothy Macmillan inspecting ARP ambulances at the Stockton depot.

210. Featured in the *Evening Gazette* in September 1970 was an old wartime sign on St John's Church Hall, Stockton. The sign, headed *Alma Street British Restaurant*, was from when the church hall was used as a feeding centre.

211. Sandbagged communal air raid shelters in Argyle Street, Middlesbrough.